Bay and Ocean

A R K   R E S T A U R A N T   C U I S I N E

Nanci Main and Jimella Lucas

LADYSMITH LTD. PUBLISHERS
SAINT LOUIS, MISSOURI

Library of Congress Catalog Card
Number 86-80066
ISBN 0-9611758-1-8

To order copies of *Bay and Ocean: Ark Restaurant
Cuisine,* send check for $21.95 ($19.95 plus $2.00
for postage and handling), U. S. currency only, to:
Ladysmith Ltd., Publishers. P. O. Box 30045,
St. Louis, MO 63119.
(Missouri residents add 6% sales tax.)

Editing, introduction, vignettes: Dick Friedrich,
Angela Harris, Elisabeth McPherson, Michael J.
Salevouris.
Art direction: Beverly Alden Bishop

Cover Art: Mark Wiseman
Book Design and Production: Wiseman Design

Photography: Eric Griswold;
p. 167 — Beverly Alden Bishop

Typesetting: Creative Graphics Center
Color Separations: Williams Litho Service, Inc.
Binding: Nicholstone Book Bindery
            Memphis, Tennessee

Printed by Fleming Printing Company
Saint Louis, Missouri

5 4 3 2 1

$19.95

Printed in U.S.A.

Dedicated to the memory of James Beard for his inspiration and support in the art of American cookery.

Also by Nanci Main & Jimella Lucas

The Ark: Cuisine of the Pacific Northwest
Ladysmith Ltd., 1983

(Paperback edition: *The Ark Restaurant Cookbook*
Penguin Books, 1985.)

Map showing the Pacific Northwest region. Locations marked include Vancouver, CANADA, Seattle, WASHINGTON, Portland, OREGON. Detailed inset map showing Willapa Bay, Oysterville, Nahcotta, Long Beach, Columbia River, Astoria, Seaside, WASHINGTON, OREGON.

2½ hrs. from Portland
3½ hrs. from Seattle

Nanci Main and Jimella Lucas, authors of *The Ark: Cuisine of the Pacific Northwest,* owner/chefs of The Ark Restaurant, and award winning chefs have prepared their second collection of recipes from their restaurant in *Bay and Ocean: Ark Restaurant Cuisine.* Listed among *Food and Wine's* Outstanding Young Chefs of America, the two trained and worked in restaurants throughout the Northwest before joining up to open the Shelburne Restaurant in Seaview, Washington, in 1980. Their national acclaim has grown consistently since James Beard wrote his first column about them in 1981. They purchased the venerable ARK Restaurant in Nahcotta, Washington, in 1982, and have, since then, been featured in *Newsweek, Town and Country, Chocolatier, The Oregonian, The Seattle Post-Intelligencer, The Boston Globe, The St. Louis Post-Dispatch,* as well as many other publications throughout the country.

All of the recipes they prepared for this book have been featured at their restaurant, The ARK, on the Nahcotta Boat Dock in Nahcotta, Washington, on the Long Beach Peninsula in southwestern Washington (206) 665-4133.

Introduction

TABLE OF CONTENTS

PENINSULA MEMORIES

The Long Beach peninsula has been an important part of my world ever since I can remember. Each summer we went to the beach, and "the beach" meant Ocean Park or Seaview or Long Beach—the three main resort towns on the narrow strip of land stretching from the mouth of the Columbia to Leadbetter Point in Willapa Bay, about thirty miles to the north.

Sixty years ago it wasn't a simple matter to get to the beach from the Portland area. Nobody went and came in a single day. Three possibilities existed. We could drive north on the old two-lane Pacific Highway to Centralia, southwest on even narrower roads through Raymond and South Bend, and down the eastern edge of Willapa Bay, a trip of more than two hundred miles. Or we could take the S. P. & S. Railroad that used to run from Portland to Astoria, cross on the ferries to Megler, and ride the narrow gauge railroad up what is now the main highway to a final stop in Nahcotta. Or we could travel in style on a riverboat from Portland to Astoria and finish the trip on the ferries and the narrow gauge train.

Once arrived at the beach we settled down to a regular routine. Two hours before low tide we went clamming; two hours before high tide we went swimming.

I'm sure bathing then was just as hazardous as it is now—just as much undertow when the tide turned, just as many logs likely to roll in, just as many deep holes into which bathers could unexpectedly plunge over their heads. And there was one minor hazard that no longer exists. Even in the shallowest water, somebody in the crowd would be sure to scream, "There's a crab on my toe!"

Crabs were plentiful in those days. My father made a special rake, rounded wire blunted on the ends, to rake them out of the crab holes left by the receding tide. He didn't always find crabs, of course, but he got them often enough to make it worth throwing the rake into the car with the clam basket.

Clamming, swimming, and occasional crabbing—those are my main memories of a peninsula vacation more than half a century ago. We did other things, of course, many still available to today's vacationers. We picked the pungent yellow sand verbena and dragged it home for sandy bouquets. We collected sand dollars down by the point. We roasted wienies and marshmallows on big driftwood fires. As children, we must have rolled in the dunes—dunes that in those days were bare of the grasses and stunted pines that cover them now—because I know I was often dunked in a round galvanized tub in the middle of the kitchen. Even the nicest cottages seldom had indoor plumbing. Part of what made a beach trip so romantic, for children at least, was the hand pump on the back porch, from which the water gushed if you pumped it hard enough; the kerosene lamps which were the only light; and the wood stoves which heated the houses and cooked the clams.

We never ate out when I was a child. My mother's cooking was better (and cheaper) than anything the few cafes could offer. We must have had vegetables now and then, and milk, and I know we used to gather the wild red huckleberries along the railroad right of way. But memory produces mostly clams, an occasional crab, and more clams, a diet of which none of us ever tired.

My children were grown and paying for their own meals before we discovered a real reason for eating out at the beach, a reason strong enough to justify a one-day drive from Portland just to eat dinner. The reason was the dining room in the Shelburne Hotel, then being run by Jimella Lucas and Nanci Main. I remember with great fondness my first meal there—sauteed salmon and caramelo. Other people have their own favorite entrees, chicken pecan or crab kasseri, sturgeon szechwan or oysters gino and their special breads and desserts such as Italian herb rolls and white chocolate mousse or triple chocolate cheese cake. But in spite of all the delectable entrees and desserts Jimella and Nanci have since provided me with, I cherish the memory of those first, perhaps because they were such a wonderful and satisfying surprise.

Nanci and Jimella do not need my praise. Nevertheless, it gives me much pleasure to write this introduction to their second book. If I have seemed to say so much about my early memories, and so little about the superb food to be found at the ARK, it is only to contrast the now with the then. Clams are much less plentiful, though the number of people looking for them has increased a thousandfold. Many of the other attractions remain the same—the lighthouses, the twenty-eight miles of driving beach, the wide windswept dunes. And in one sense, the highlight of a beach trip still the same—a lot of eating you can't get back home. The emphasis, however, has shifted. For most of us nowadays, it's not the fried clams that tasted so wonderful, partly because we had dug and cleaned them ourselves—it's the chance to have a really first-rate dinner at the ARK. Even for the nights we stay at home, it's the opportunity to recreate some of the ARK's recipes in our own kitchens, so I welcome this second cookbook, as will all those cooks across the country who benefitted from the first one.

Here's to Jimella and Nanci, who have changed the focus of a trip to the beach!

Elisabeth McPherson
Vancouver, Washington, and
Long Beach, Washington

THE CHEFS AND THE ARK

"How did you decide to put a restaurant way out here?" The question comes up often at the ARK. Three hours from Seattle, over two from Portland, the ARK sits on the northern half of a peninsula that serves as home to a few thousand hardy souls who work hard, value their independence, love the ocean and have made their peace with the rain and clouds. So how does The ARK, lauded in the *Boston Globe, Chicago Tribune, St. Louis Post-Dispatch, Washington Post, Town and Country Magazine* and *Newsweek Magazine*—to name but a few of the hundreds nationally—come to be off in this corner of the country?

To understand, it helps to know something about the fiercely independent Nanci Main and Jimella Lucas. They both weigh their decisions carefully, but make those decisions firmly. In spite of their genius in marketing, they refuse to court success by compromising their commitment to the quality of their art. When the opportunity to open their place presented itself on the Long Beach peninsula, they had the serenely inflexible faith in themselves that characterizes most artists.

The location that seems so out of the way is, in fact, just right: the ocean, the bay, and the Columbia River guarantee the freshest and finest oysters, crab, sturgeon, salmon, crawfish, tuna, halibut, clams. The lava-rich soil produces an abundance of vegetables and fruits: here the blackberries and bright red huckleberries grow profusely on their own, while the strawberries and raspberries reward their growers with a lush sweetness and juiciness unknown to the rest of the world. Nowhere in the world is the chicken juicier with a rich butter flavor, nowhere is the veal more tender, more rich. The spinach, the romaine lettuce have no bitterness; the carrots, beets and peas crunch sweetly. Even the red of the radish and the green of the sugar pea reflect a kind of popping firmness and mild flavor. And the nearby cities of Portland and Seattle provide sources for the finest chocolates, freshest spices and richest oils from all over the planet.

When you eat at the ARK, you benefit from all this bounty as well as from the artistry of Main and Lucas. From the first, when you enter their restaurant, you are in their hands. The decor is theirs, the arrangements of flowers, the color of the carpet, the precise placement of the table settings—all reflect their attention to detail and their taste. When you are seated by the hostess, it may well be Nanci Main herself who describes the evening's specials; if it isn't, her voice is certainly reflected in the hostess' or host's greeting to you. Your wine will be opened and poured according to their instructions in order to enhance your enjoyment. And your plate will reflect Jimella Lucas' aesthetic commitment to visual as well as culinary taste. It will be colorful, balanced, and prepared moments before—just for you.

This is how they started their restaurant just a few years ago. And because their skills and talents mixed so gracefully with the locale, they attracted the attention of folks from Portland, Seattle and down the coast in Oregon. People came to know them for their imaginative use of the freshest fish, the best of the locally grown produce, and the most succulent local veal, chicken and beef.

One of the better known visitors to the coast of Oregon heard of them one day and decided to see what the fuss was all about. He had been born and raised in Gearhart, Oregon, but left to make his name in New York. He had worked hard at his craft and soon became known from San Francisco to Europe. But in spite of his fame, James Beard never forgot where he had come from.

He never forgot the Dungeness crab, the crayfish, the mussels and salmon; he cherished in his memory the Oregon strawberries, the mushrooms, the wild berries, the peas and other vegetables from his youth. And for years, every time he made one of his periodic return visits, he looked in vain for some place that would give the gifts from the sea their due.

In the first ARK cookbook, Mr. Beard spoke of his delight in finding Nanci and Jimella. He raved about the bounty glorified by these women in their restaurant. He talked of their "new creativity," their "variety and goodness." He celebrated Jimella's "taste. She has imagination and she is able to create new and exciting menus." Nanci, he said, "has the gift of charming the ovens as a pastry cook. She has imagination. She complements Jimella's creativity with her own."

"Now," Mr. Beard wrote at about the time of his eightieth birthday party at the Four Seasons in New York, eaters had the "opportunity to revel in some of the goodies, not only the fish but the chanterelle and the other wild mushrooms and the vegetables that abound in the sandy soil and have a quality that one seldom finds anywhere else." He praised the "new ways with fish, new ways with shell fish and new ideas," that he found in their restaurant and in their first cookbook.

He spoke also of his attempts to "blow the trumpet and wave the banners." He claimed (too modestly, according to Nanci and Jimella) that "I think I enlisted a small army of co-boosters who spread the word." In fact, what he had done was far more.

He had published reviews of the restaurant in over 100 newspapers around the USA and Canada. He visited often, giving them his support, his encouragement, his advice, his love.

Often, he asked them to visit him in New York. And in his seventy-ninth year, they were able to accept the invitation. They visited him, ate at his favorite places and drew from his personal strength. They returned to the West Coast energized—as they always were—by this man's intelligence, his taste, his warmth and generosity—and his commitment to excellent American regional cuisine.

He returned to the ARK to eat twice more: once for nearly a week. He ate salmon cheeks and sturgeon and fresh peach marzipan tart. He was delighted with Nanci's strawberry shortcake—made from his mother's recipe. And when he left, he left reluctantly.

*   *   *   *   *   *   *   *   *   *

James Beard has left behind a large culinary following. Diners and chefs across the land remember him and his contributions to all who love to eat and love to work with food. Nanci Main and Jimella Lucas carry on, cooking in his tradition, grateful for his contribution.

(continued)

They remember this kind man, this wise man who touched them so briefly but so deeply. The following recipe is meant to honor the man and his work. To say thank you from Nanci Main and Jimella Lucas, from the ARK. "The recipe was created in honor of James Beard for a tribute dinner in Portland, Oregon, May 7, 1985 with the first vine-ready Oregon strawberries of the season—the berries he loved so much."—Jimella Lucas

STRAWBERRY GARLIC VINAIGRETTE FOR JAMES BEARD

walnuts	*salt*	*olive oil*
garlic	*black pepper*	*salad oil*
green onions	*lemon*	*egg*
parsley	*strawberries*	
dijon mustard	*red wine vinegar*	

Blend thoroughly **2 T walnuts, 10 cloves garlic, 2 sliced green onions, 1 T chopped parsley, 1 T dijon mustard, pinch salt, 3 twists of peppermill, strained juice of 2 lemons, 1 c washed sliced strawberries,* 3 to 4 T red wine vinegar.*** With machine running, add **1 c olive oil, 1 c salad oil.** Finally add **1 egg** to smooth out texture.

Yield: 3 cups

T I P S

Strawberries should be *very* ripe: perhaps riper even than you would ordinarily eat.

Amount of vinegar depends on the fullness of the berries. Start with 3 T, then adjust.

With love, *Nanci Jimella*

How To Use This Book

Many people collect cookbooks just to have them and that's fine. Many others have cookbooks simply to read them. And that's fine too. *Bay and Ocean*, as you know, is beautiful simply to look at and is enjoyable reading. But we recommend that you let this book add a new dimension to your cooking and eating. The recipes work in home kitchens—we know; we've used them.

Here are a few areas to pay special attention to:

1. Just as the ARK chefs do, use only the finest ingredients. Don't use what grocery stores label "cooking wine." Don't cook with any wine you wouldn't drink.

Use the finest chocolate available to you; Chef Main uses fine Belgian chocolate. Use the freshest possible herbs, vegetables and fruits. In fact, if you are preparing a dish that calls for one kind of berry and good ones are unavailable, switch to another fruit.

2. Experiment. Read the recipe and if it comes to you that you might like a bit more garlic or you want honey instead of sugar, make the change. Your food should reflect your preferences. The recipes are guides, not limits, to your imagination.

3. Be ready when you start to put the ingredients together. Have *all* the ingredients at hand: the shallots chopped, the dijon measured, the eggs at room temperature. Have the flour and sugar measured, the chocolate shredded. Then the execution of the dish becomes an easy matter, even one which your guests can watch.

4. Following are some terms you may find unfamiliar:

thump—Rap bread sharply with a knuckle. If it sounds hollow, it is done.

proof—Let yeast sponge or dough rise.

dust—Gently fondle oysters, chicken, fish, whatever, in handfuls of flour. Shake off all excess, leaving only shadow of flour.

deglaze—Pour wine or liquor into a hot pan to loosen the residue in the pan.

poach—Cook in water or stock.

saute—After heating oil in pan to high heat, place food in it to cook.

marry—Allow elements in a sauce to blend, to come together.

bind—Hold together.

pipe—Use a pastry cone to handle dough with more control, to fill a parfait glass, or, with tips of varying shape, to decorate a dessert.

carmelize—Bring sauce to caramel thickness.

5. Have ingredients you use often on hand all the time: stocks, butter, breadcrumbs, sauces. Make them in season and freeze.

And don't ever be caught without genache.

OVERTURE

Early this morning, about 4:30, in fact, the crumbs from last night's dinners got vacuumed from the floor, the hard floors were cleaned, the windows were washed, sills dusted and polished as was the rest of the wood. Since 9:00 a.m., Rose and Nanci have been baking bread, muffins, making Swedish Cream, bread pudding and the night's special desserts.

4:30 in the afternoon. Tamara and Amy have chopped mushrooms, white and green onions, parsley, diced tomatoes, shucked peas, cleaned calamari, prawns, opened and rinsed oysters and are now grating the Kasseri, gruyere, and parmesan cheese. Meanwhile, Anne has the evening's salad dressings ready, as well as the salad station's condiments, the carrots and cucumbers and cherry tomatoes and lettuces and red cabbage, cocktail sauce, the oil and vinegar, the butter for the evening's breads and toasts. She has the lemons sliced for the water glasses and cut lemon wedges. She moves back to the bakery to pick up the breads fresh from the ovens. Teresa, meanwhile, has been flying back and forth doing whatever Tamara and Amy and Anne haven't the time for. The banter, the jokes, the teasing come easy in this kitchen: shouts back and forth alternate with Jimella's requests, orders and questions. "Teresa, could you get the appetizers set up? Tamara, go ahead, get the lettuce ready." "Hey Jimella, you want those beets sliced thinner?" "I'll never understand how Rose got up this morning. Watch out for her coming around the corner· there." "Who's doing the dessert trays here?" "Ooowheee. I saw you riding around showing off that new car. Pretty slick." "Look out, here comes Rose." "I was just driving to my Mom's house." Much belly laughing.

Out front, Debbie, tonight's early waitress, zips about, changing flowers, making sure there is plenty of water in the vases, arranging the placemats and silverware and plates and glasses *precisely*, just so, putting the evening's white wines into the front cooler, folding napkins, arranging bread baskets, making sure the salt and pepper are filled to the right level and arranged on the tables exactly the way Nanci wants them. The first coffee is prepared; the ice bin, filled; the espresso machine, started.

Karen is in the bar tonight; it's Jan's night off. She has the wines set up, fruits for drinks cut, sliced, wedged. As she rushes through with coffee and bar ice, someone shouts, "Hey Karen, can you fix a Smith and Wesson? My mother's coming in tonight." (Everyone likes to tease the bartenders with strange requests—gin and pepsi, scotch and campari.) Karen responds, but no one can hear; she rushes to do the final touches. In the lounge or at table, everything has a place, a very specific, exact place. And everything is in its place.

4:45. Lots of movement and clatter in the kitchen; it's controlled chaos, everyone hurrying with last moment preparations. In the middle of it all, Jimella enters with two lavendar roses, just opening. She puts them in a cocktail glass and sets the small arrangement up by the line. She looks at them, steps back a foot, looks at them again, goes up to them, fusses with them a bit, steps back. Smiles. Cheryl has fixed the rice, the 4 egg bearnaise, the 4 egg hollandaise, moved in the evening's vegetables. Greg quietly flours (lightly) the oysters and lays them out in neat rows, his hands very gently fondling these jewels from Willapa bay.

4:50. Then, suddenly, no one's talking. Just a lot of movement. A pan bangs occasionally. Chris stands ready at the dishwasher, watching. Cheryl puts on her chef's hat. Jimella enters from the left. No sandals now. Work shoes. Chef's hat on.

4:55. Even the movement stops. The waitresses have their trays ready—each has poured a little water on a napkin to keep it from slipping on the tray. Coffee ready. Tables set. The blackboard with the evening's specials is on its easel. April notes several early arrivals outside by the door. She puts on a tape of Mozart. Moves quietly to the kitchen. She looks to Jimella.

"Ready? It's five."

"Ready."

Techniques for
Ark Cooking

AN OYSTER'S
LAMENT

It ain't easy being an oyster. First, oysters can reproduce only when the temperature of their water stays within a certain range. Then the oyster enters the larval stage when it spends 2 to 3 weeks swimming around toward light sources. The animals already have their two shells but are so tiny that 500 of them in a row would make a line only one inch long. To make this connection they actually grow an appendage, a foot, with a glue gland at the end. Then the individual animal must reach out until it finds something solid.

The next stage in the oyster's growth, the one day metamorphosis, is most critical for survival. From 70% to 90% of the larval oysters do not make it through this stage. The survivors, or spat, grow into what most people would recognize as oysters. Oysters may attach to any of a number of objects in the water but most commonly attach to old oyster shells: if the oysters cannot attach, they rarely, if ever, survive.

Once the oysters have attached themselves, they grow by extracting nutrients from the water which flows constantly through their shells: their food comes to them. As stationary animals, however, they are at the mercy of various kinds of threats: the vagaries of temperature and currents in the water may affect their food source and a variety of predators threaten them. Natural enemies of oysters (aside from humans who love their taste) include starfish, not a major problem in the Northwest beds, crabs, and Japanese oyster drills (tiny snails which drill through the oyster's shell and nibble at the muscle until the shell pops open).

Oysters need cold weather to grow. All of their energy is converted into glycogen and they become plump and firm—the way we like to eat them. As the weather and water temperature warm up, the oyster's energy diverts to the development of reproductive products. The oyster may lose up to 30% of its body weight during this time—it's busy preserving its species, not itself.

OYSTER SHUCKING

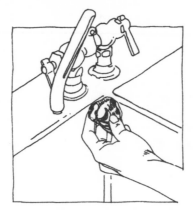

Wash carefully — especially the hole.

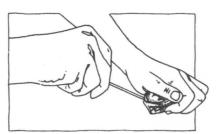

Insert knife into the hole.

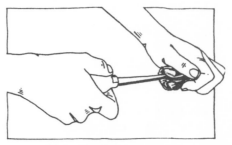

Twist knife to open.

OYSTERS WITH ITALIAN BREAD CRUMBS

oysters

Italian bread
crumbs

lemon

butter

parmesan

Oven: 425°

Place **oyster** in half shell. Top with
1 T Italian bread crumbs, squeeze of
lemon, dribble of **clarified butter,** sprinkle
of **parmesan.**

Bake for 3 to 4 minutes or place under
broiler.*

T   I   P   S

The bread crumbs may burn if too close to
flame.

ITALIAN BREAD CRUMBS

garlic

bread

parsley

parmesan

tabasco

Grind in food processor or blender **1 clove
garlic,** adding **2 slices day old bread** till
finely ground. Add **2 sprigs parsley** without
stems, **1 T grated parmesan, 1 dash
tabasco.**

Yield: 1½ cups

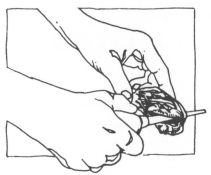

Move knife the length of oyster
opening all the way.

OYSTERS
WITH SPINACH SAUCE

spinach

garlic

shallots

butter

mushrooms

lemon

flour

anisette

cream

oysters

Oven: 425°

Blanch **5 c fresh spinach** (tightly packed).
Chop in food processor. Saute **1 t minced
garlic, 1 t minced shallots** in
¼ c clarified butter.* Add **¼ c chopped
mushrooms,** then spinach. Squeeze
½ lemon over mixture. Sprinkle **½ t flour**
into liquid. Deglaze with **anisette.** Add **2 T
heavy cream.** Cook until sauce comes
together.

Place **18 to 24 oysters** in half shells. Top
with 1 to 2 T spinach mixture. Bake for 4 to
5 minutes.

T I P S

For clarified butter technique, see p. 34.

Serves: 6

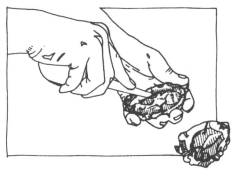

Slide knife gently under the oyster separating it from the shell.

OYSTERS GINO

oysters
gino sauce

Oven: 425°

Place **oysters on half shell** on rock salt in iron pan. Place **1 to 2 T gino sauce** on each oyster. Bake for 12 to 15 minutes.

T I P S

For gino sauce, see p. 181.

OYSTERS WITH PEPPER PAN SAUCE

oysters
pepper pan sauce

Oven: 425°

Place **oysters on the half shell** on a bed of rock salt in an iron pan. Put **1 to 2 T pepper pan sauce*** on each oyster. Bake for 12 to 15 minutes.

T I P S

For pepper pan sauce recipe, see p. 171.

CLARIFIED BUTTER

butter
safflower oil

Put **1 lb butter** in glass measuring cup or bowl. Add **⅓ c safflower oil.** * Put in pan of water; bring water to boil. Cook at least 30 minutes over medium low heat till butter melts and fat moves to top, whey to bottom. Skim fat off top;* don't worry about the whey in bottom. Use clear butter oil from top.

Keep this tightly covered in refrigerator; it will last as long as butter would.

T I P S

The addition of the oil tempers the burning potential of the butter. Any light vegetable oil will work.

Chill clarified butter to making skimming easier.

ROUX

butter
flour

Melt **1 c butter;** let it start to bubble.* Add **1½ c flour,** one spoonful at a time, stirring, then adding. Cook on low heat 5 to 10 minutes, stirring.

Cool, cover tightly, store in refrigerator.

T I P S

Be sure butter is bubbling before adding flour.

CANDIED ROSE PETALS

egg whites
rose petals
sugar

Gently whip **3 egg whites** until bubbly and thinned. Dip **fresh rose petals;** smooth through fingers to remove excess egg white. Lay petals in bowl of **superfine sugar;** shake gently. Turn over and dip in sugar again till just coated.* Shake off excess.

Lay petals on parchment paper to dry at room temperature. Dry on one side for several hours, turn over. Store in airtight container when dried completely.

T I P S

Avoid clumping of sugar.

CREME FRAICHE

cream
buttermilk

Fold together **2 c heavy cream, 2 T buttermilk.** Place in glass jar. Cover jar lightly with cheese cloth. Put jar in gas oven* with pilot overnight (12 hours).

T I P S

With an electric oven, pre-heat oven to lowest setting. Turn oven off, put jar inside. Do not open oven till time is up. Or set oven at low and keep door open.

SIMPLE SYRUP

sugar
water

Combine **1 c sugar** and **1 c water.** Heat until sugar is dissolved.

BEAR CLAW ASSEMBLY

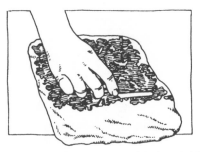

Spread walnut mixture on two thirds of 12" by 18" rolled out dough.

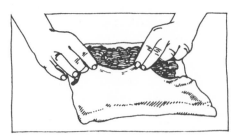

Fold third without walnut mixture back over.

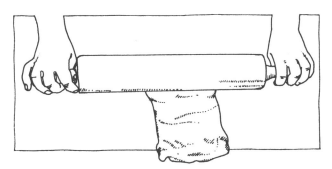

After folding over last third, roll out to flatten.

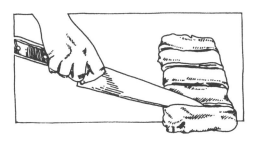

Slice dough into 12 even bear claws.

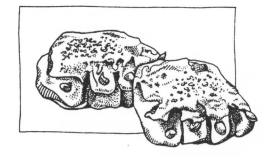

BEAR CLAWS

beaver bread
dough
walnuts
bread crumbs
brown sugar
cinnamon
butter
honey
milk
egg
powdered sugar
vanilla

Oven: 350°

Let **one recipe beaver bread dough*** rise until doubled in size. Punch down and roll out into rectangle 12" x 18".

Spread ⅔ of rectangle (lengthwise) with mixture of **3 c finely chopped walnuts, 1 c fine bread crumbs, 2 c brown sugar, 2 t cinnamon, ½ c melted butter, ¾ c honey.**

Fold uncovered ⅓ of dough over middle of walnut mixture. Fold over again forming rectangle 6" x 12". Pinch ends. Roll out and flatten. Cut into 12 equal rectangles. On long side of each individual roll, cut 3 slits, ⅔ into bear claw. Pull the sections apart, forming the bear's claws.

Place on parchment covered baking sheet. Let rise for 15 to 20 minutes. Brush with glaze made of **¼ c milk** and **1 egg.** Bake for 30 minutes. Remove from oven.

Frost while still warm with glaze made by combining **1 c sifted powdered sugar, 2 T softened butter, ½ t vanilla,** and **4 t milk** to make glaze thick.

T I P S

For Beaver Bread recipe, see page 70.

Whole almonds can be used to decorate bear claws by pressing almonds deep into claws before proofing.

Yield: 12

Salmon Filleting

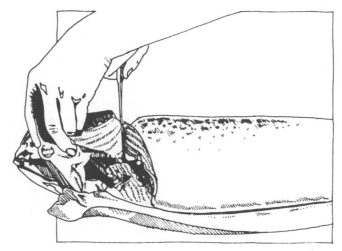

Cut tail from body. Cut head, behind gills, from body. Clear all fins.

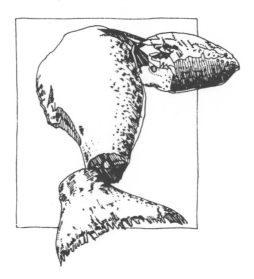

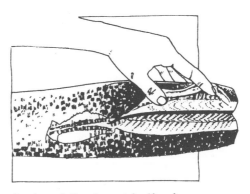

At dorsal fin, insert knife along
the top of the bone until the tip
hits the spinal column. Clear top
fillet. Then work knife up
towards head or neck area. Use
same procedure toward tail.

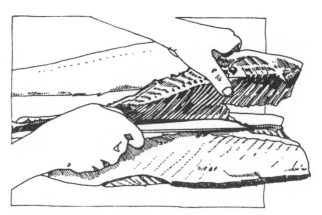

With the tip of your knife, clear spinal
column. Then, starting at the neck, pull the
knife at a 45° angle over the top of the rib
bones to clear fillet. To clear bottom fillet
insert knife at the tail using the spinal column as a guide line and work out towards
top of fish. To clear the rack start at the
neck and draw the knife along the rib
cage.

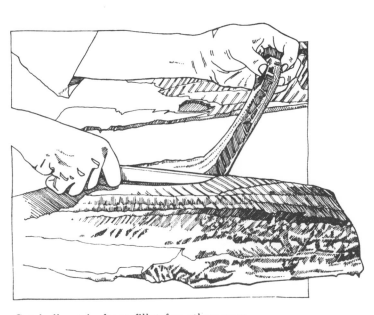

Cut belly strip from fillet for other uses.

Brunch at the Ark

ON THE LINE

The heart of any restaurant kitchen is the line—where all the prep work comes together to create each diner's meal. It's no different at the ARK.

Most people would not expect to find a woman with a Master's degree in social work and ten years in the field working as a cook in Nahcotta, Washington. Cheryl doesn't see her move as strange: she sees both social work and cooking as nurturing activities. In fact, before she ever came to the ARK, she had a small catering business in Seattle that she ran while she still worked at community organizing. She believes that her work as a line chef allows her to demonstrate an idea that had been forming for some time: that taking responsibility for nurturing activities can be an empowering act; it does not have to reflect the mere acceptance of a predetermined role.

Cheryl ended up on the line at the ARK by proposing an independent apprenticeship there so that she could learn and work in a place where her special skills and interests might be most appreciated and enhanced. She describes her year-long commitment to the ARK as a "gift to myself."

Anne, an apprentice, started her college career at Cornell University as a political science major—"Politics is just part of my family." But one day she realized that she wanted to study something of her own that she "could really do," so she took her experience as the youngest of eight children (the one who got to do the cooking) and her background in waitressing and headed over to the hotel and restaurant management school at Cornell. Good-bye political science.

(continued)

From there she transferred to the New England Culinary Institute which requires two six month apprenticeships for graduation. So, wanting to be on the West coast, and wanting to work with women, she applied at the ARK. To her delight, she found what she had hoped for. And a good deal more.

BLUEBERRY MUFFIN BREAD

This surprising bread hits the spot on a cloudy autumn day. Spread the still warm bread with butter and let it melt. Pour yourself a big glass of milk and you'll be back in your grandmother's kitchen. (That's if you're lucky enough to have a grandmother who can bake as well as Chef Main.)

flour
baking powder
salt
nutmeg
cinnamon
sugar
butter
eggs
canned pumpkin
buttermilk
yellow cornmeal
blueberries
walnuts
lemon rind

Oven: 350°

Sift **1½ c flour** with **1 T baking powder, 1 t salt, ½ t nutmeg, ½ t cinnamon.** Set aside.

Beat together **½ c sugar, ¼ c soft butter,** and **2 eggs** until smooth.

Add **1 c canned pumpkin, ½ c buttermilk, 1 c yellow cornmeal.** Beat until smooth. Stir in dry mixture.

Fold in **1 c blueberries, 1 c coarsely chopped walnuts, ½ t grated lemon rind.**

Spread evenly into a greased 9" x 5" loaf pan.

Bake for 1 hour.

Yield: 1 loaf

SEAFOOD BENEDICT

For many of the ARK's regulars, Seafood Benedict for Sunday Brunch by the bay is the only way to start the week. Listening to the gentle sounds of one of the musicians who play every week, sipping on a Champagne Cocktail and tasting this rich seafood dish make the coming work week seem very far away.

fish
butter
mushrooms
white onion
garlic
tabasco
lemon
salt
white pepper
elegant cheese sauce
sherry
tomato
green onion
garlic toast
egg
hollandaise sauce

For each serving cut **4 oz fish*** into ½" to ¾" chunks and add to skillet containing **2 to 3 T clarified butter.*** Add **⅓ c sliced mushrooms, ¼ c thinly sliced white onion, ½ t garlic, 1 dash tabasco,** squeeze of **1 wedge of lemon, salt** and **white pepper to taste.** Cook for 2 to 3 minutes, shaking pan to keep fish from sticking. Turn the fish.

Add **2 T elegant cheese sauce.***

Deglaze with **¼ c sherry.** Allow ingredients to marry.

Add **1½ t diced tomato, 1½ t chopped green onions.**

Place mixture on **slice of toasted garlic bread.** Top with **1 poached egg** and **dollop of hollandaise sauce.***

T I P S

A combination of any three of the following fish: halibut, salmon, sturgeon, ling cod. For a deluxe Seafood Benedict, use little scallops, salmon, ling cod and at the last minute, add 2 oz cocktail shrimp.

For clarified butter technique, see p. 34.

For elegant cheese sauce recipe, see p. 178.

For hollandaise sauce recipe, see p. 182.

Serve garnished with fruit.

Recipe is per serving; multiply as needed.

SEAFOOD JOE

The west side of the peninsula has a band of dark grey clouds that shroud the day as you drive north from Ilwaco on your way to the ARK. As you reach Ocean Park and turn right to go east toward Willapa Bay, you glide through ghostly clouds wisping across the road. Then, just as you reach Sandridge road, the blue sky opens over the waters of the largest unpolluted estuary in the United States; in the distance the hills on the other side of the water urge their tops above the cloud cover, making a jagged dark ribbon over the white cloud bank. And soon, you'll be eating: Seafood Joe or Chicken Livers Mediterranean—or a Hangtown Fry made as only Jimella makes this traditional dish with oysters picked from the bay glistening right outside your window. Another week launched perfectly—by eating at the ARK.

seafood bits
butter
mushrooms
lemon
salt
pepper
tabasco
garlic
shallots
spinach
egg
dry vermouth
garlic toast

For each serving, saute 6 or more **seafood bits*** in **2 T clarified butter*** with ⅓ c **sliced mushrooms.** Add **juice 1 lemon wedge, salt, pepper** to taste, **1 shot tabasco, ½ t minced garlic, ½ t minced shallot.** Saute till fish flakes—total cooking time about 4 to 5 minutes depending on thickness of fish.

Toward end, add **½ c chopped fresh spinach bound with 1 whipped egg.** Deglaze with **¼ c dry vermouth.**

Serve open faced on toasted **garlic bread.**

T I P S

For seafood bits, cut into ½" cubes, salmon, halibut, ling cod, perch, scallops, prawns, or any other preferred fish.

For clarified butter technique, see p. 34.

Recipe is per serving; multiply as needed.

*E*ven people in the stone age ate salmon. The regal fish's bones have been found in caves in southern Europe where Old Stone Age humans lived. In fact, in the floor of the Grotto du Poisson near Les Eyzies, France, there remains a bas relief from the stone age depicting the anatomy of the salmon with remarkable accuracy.

BAKED AVOCADO WITH SCALLOPS AND COGNAC SAUCE

When you arrive at your table you'll certainly notice Robert's handiwork: the table is perfectly set: placemat, precisely set one inch from the table's edge; silverware, according to traditional arrangement; bread plate, middle left of top of placemat; wine glass, top right hand corner; salt to the right, pepper to the left; candle set center. Not a crumb in sight. And now he comes with water, served over ice with a slice of lemon—one of those touches that make dinner special at the ARK. Robert, a big man, moves easily about the dining room, presenting desserts confidently, professionally. Not exactly the stereotypical ex-marine, Robert has also served as a giant ARK Easter bunny, perhaps the biggest visible rabbit in the Pacific Northwest. Additionally, at the Garlic Festival, Robert was dressed as the world's largest garlic clove. "I'm having a good time, are you?" both startled and cheered many a guest at the festival during the rain that morning.

scallops	Oven: 425°
fish stock	Poach **2½ lbs fresh Oregon or bay**
celery	**scallops*** in **fish stock*** for 3 to 4
green onion	minutes. Remove from liquid and cool.
mushrooms	Toss scallops with **½ c diced celery,**
lemon	**½ sliced green onion, ¾ c sliced**
salt	**mushrooms, juice of 1 lemon, salt and**
pepper	**pepper, ⅓ c parmesan.**
parmesan	In saucepan combine **2 c fish stock, 1 c**
fish stock	**heavy cream, salt and white pepper** to
heavy cream	taste, **3 dashes tabasco, 2 to 3 T dijon**
tabasco	**mustard, 1 t worchestershire.** Heat until
dijon mustard	warm enough to accept **4 to 5 T roux.*** Add
worcestershire	**⅓ c cognac.** Cook 4 to 5 minutes more.
roux	Mix sauce into scallop mixture.
cognac	

avocados
italian bread
crumbs
butter

Halve **6 large ripe avocados.** Place
2 to 3 T scallop filling into each cavity.
Sprinkle with generous topping of **Italian
bread crumbs.*** Drizzle **clarified butter***
over top.

Bake for 12 to 15 minutes, until avocado is
warm and bread crumbs are browned.

T I P S

Use tiny bay scallops.

For fish stock recipe, see p. 194.

For roux recipe, see p. 34.

For Italian bread crumb recipe, see p. 31.

For clarified butter recipe, see p. 34.

Serve topped with generous dollop of
hollandaise for an especially decadent treat.
For hollandaise recipe, see p. 182.

Serve as a brunch entree with fruit and fennel
potatos or as an appetizer with a slightly
smaller amount of scallop filling and no
hollandaise.

Serves 12 but filling can be kept for several
days and servings can be made up a few
at a time.

BRIOCHE

Put a basket of brioche on the table and any meal becomes a feast.

sugar	Oven: 400°
yeast	Place **6 T sugar, 3 cakes live yeast**
milk	(1½ oz) in **1 c warm milk.** Whip to dissolve.
salt	Mix in **¾ t salt, 3 beaten eggs.** Add **¼ lb**
eggs	**butter,** softened, and **5 c flour.** Knead for
butter	10 minutes in mixer (15 minutes by hand*),
flour	until dough is shiny, satiny, and smooth.
water	Place in bowl, cover with plastic wrap and let rise until doubled, 1 to 1½ hours.

Divide dough into 15 to 18 equal rolls. Place in well-greased muffin tins or brioche pans. Proof for 30 minutes or until rolls are not quite doubled in size. After 15 minutes, brush with egg wash made of **1 egg** and **1 t water.***

Bake for 20 to 30 minutes. When brioche begin to brown, brush quickly with same egg wash.

T I P S

When kneading, lift the dough high and throw vigorously onto the work table. This will help develop the dough and produce its smooth satiny texture.

Be careful that no egg wash drips down inside pans since it will cause rolls to stick.

Yield: 15 to 18 rolls

POACHED SCALLOP SALAD WITH PROSCIUTTO AND PEAS

Chef Lucas specializes in seafood and occasionally her Italian ancestry shows through in one of her recipes: witness the presence of prosciutto in this salad.

fish stock
white wine
scallops
shelled peas
prosciutto
celery
strawberry garlic vinaigrette
celery seed
lettuce
walnuts
avocado
strawberries

Bring to boil **3 c fish stock,* 3 c white wine;** add **1 lb fresh Oregon or sea scallops.** Cook for 3 to 4 minutes.* Remove to colander; drop ice over them and refrigerate immediately.*

When cool, mix together with **1 c shelled peas, 1 to 2 oz chopped prosciutto, 1 chopped rib celery.** Toss with **¼ c strawberry garlic vinaigrette,* ¼ t celery seed.** Set aside for 1 to 2 hours.

Lay each serving on a bed of **lettuce;** to each serving add dollop of **1 T strawberry garlic vinaigrette.** Garnish with **chopped walnuts, quartered avocado** and **strawberries.**

T I P S

For fish stock recipe, see p. 194.

Do not overcook; better to have them on the underdone side.

If you have poached them in a colander or drainer to start with, you don't have to scoop them with a slotted spoon.

For strawberry garlic vinaigrette recipe, see p. 19.

Serves: 4

ORANGE HONEY NUT BREAD

Tuesday morning. 60 degrees. Not a cloud to be seen. Nanci reviewing messages from the answering machine. Tom Zimmerman and his father are making the produce and honey delivery. Does Nanci want to buy her honey in five gallon buckets? Rose's back wouldn't appreciate the weight. How about a darker honey for the orange honey nut bread? It'd make it better. OK. Let's try it.

Tom goes by with a basket of beets—enormous greens, not a mark or a break in the leaves. Nanci opens a pea shell and tastes the peas. They pop, so fresh. These'll be fine.

Mr. Zimmerman in his worn leather hat, white beard, plaid shirt tells Nanci about the process of honey making—cooking kills the enzymes—larger commercial places call the process pasteurization. Honey with dead enzymes. Not for Nanci. She'll try the darker honey; she'll continue to get the gallon jars instead of the five gallon tubs. And maybe she'll make Orange Honey Nut Bread today.

honey	Oven: 350°
shortening	Cream **1 c honey, 2 T shortening** for 1
egg	minute at medium speed. Add **1 beaten egg.**
flour	Sift **2⅔ c flour** with **2½ t baking powder,**
baking powder	**½ t baking soda, ½ t salt.**
baking soda	Add flour mixture to creamed mixture
salt	alternately with **¾ c orange juice.**
orange juice	Stir in **1 c chopped nuts** and **1½ T grated**
chopped nuts	**orange peel.**
orange peel	Bake in greased loaf pan for 60 minutes.
	Yield: 1 loaf

CHICKEN LIVERS MEDITERRANEAN

Chicken liver lovers will not be disappointed with this saute dish and even those who don't usually select chicken livers will be delighted with the delicate flavor of this brunch selection.

chicken livers
flour
butter
salt
pepper
mushrooms
onion
garlic
tabasco
madeira
tomato
green onions
sour cream
parsley

For each serving saute **4 to 6 oz lightly floured* chicken livers** in **4 T hot clarified butter.* Salt, pepper** to taste. When they start to brown, turn. Add **¼ c sliced mushrooms, 1 T thinly sliced white onion, ½ t minced garlic, 2 shots tabasco.**

As garlic starts to brown, deglaze with **¼ c madeira.** Cook till just starting to firm, about 3 minutes, then add another **¼ c madeira.**

Add 1 **T diced tomato** and **1 t sliced green onions** just before removing from heat.

Serve with a dollop of **sour cream** and sprinkling of **chopped fresh parsley.**

T I P S

Be sure to shake off excess flour to prevent burning.

For clarified butter technique, see p. 34.

Recipe is per serving; multiply as needed.

Many of the place names on the peninsula obviously describe the geography of the area— Long Beach, Ocean Park, Oysterville, North Head, and the bay's original name, Shoalwater.

The name of Cape Disappointment reflects the feelings of the British trader John Meares. In 1788, Meares failed to find the entrance to the Great River of the West and decided it didn't exist. He named Deception Bay on the same trip.

Peacock Spit, cause of so many ship wrecks, got its name from the U. S. sloop of war, the Peacock, which went aground on the sands in 1841.

Bay and Ocean

NOTES

Favorites from the Ark Bakery

NAHCOTTA AND ITS NEIGHBORS

The town of Nahcotta was created about 1889 when it became the terminus for the new narrow gauge railroad. Before the line was finished, two of the railroad's major stockholders, Lewis Loomis and B. A. Seaborg, quarreled. Seaborg bought land on one side of the track and established a town called Sealand, built a hotel, and got a post office. Loomis started a town on the other side, called it Nahcotta, and built his own hotel, but it was four years before Nahcotta residents persuaded a Democratic administration in Olympia to give it the post office. A wharf was built into the bay so lumber could be loaded on the trains; stores opened, houses were built. Then about twenty years after Nahcotta was founded, one of the hotels caught fire and the town was reduced to ashes. Now it is distinguished only for its wharf, its boat moorage, its enormous hill of oyster shells, its oyster processing plant, and, of course, the ARK restaurant.

Across the peninsula, the town of Ocean Park began quite sedately. About 1884, ten Methodist ministers and ten laymen acquired 140 acres of land there and formed the Methodist Camp Meeting Association. The idea was to combine a summer resort, where people could camp, with a revival meeting, where they could worship. Soon after the association was formed, lots were sold to a few outsiders, but every deed carried restrictions against saloons, gambling houses, and other forms of wickedness. Even today, when people buy homes in Ocean Park they must often sign a statement agreeing that they will not sell liquor.

Oysterville, a scattered collection of ten or twelve historic houses three miles north of Nahcotta, is all that's left of the first non-Indian settlement on the peninsula. Established in 1854 by Clarke, Espy and the Crellins, the town quickly grew to more than five hundred residents and at least five saloons catering to those who worked in the oysters.

CRANBERRY NUT COOKIES

These chewy, moist cookies are based on a recipe from Jean Brennan, Kaaren's mother. Chef Main makes them each year for the Cranberry Festival in Ilwaco where they're always a favorite. With their delicate pink color and white chocolate topping, they look as good as they taste when served as part of a holiday tray.

butter
sugar
brown sugar
flour
baking powder
salt
milk
vanilla
candied fruit
grated orange peel
cranberries
walnuts
filberts
white chocolate

Oven: 350°

Cream together **½ c butter, 1 c sugar, ¾ c brown sugar.** Sift together **3 c all-purpose flour, 1 t baking powder, ½ t salt.**

Add dry ingredients to butter mixture alternately with **⅓ c milk,** scraping bowl often. Add **1 t vanilla.** Combine **½ c candied fruit, 1 T grated orange peel, 2½ c chopped cranberries,* 1 c chopped walnuts,* 1 c chopped filberts.**

Fold fruit and nut mixture into rest of ingredients. Drop by spoonfuls* onto lined baking sheet. Bake for 15 minutes, until cookies begin to turn golden on sides but remain moist.

When cookies have cooled, shred and melt over hot water **4 oz white chocolate*** using a whisk to break down lumps as chocolate melts. Invert cookies over melted white chocolate and dip top to cover about half the top with the chocolate.* Decorate with a walnut half, or several pieces of candied fruit.*

Freeze cranberries and chop in a food processor for best results.

Chef Main likes walnuts and filberts in combination, but 2 c of either one works.

A 1 oz ice cream scoop makes an ideal cookie size.

White chocolate grates well when chilled first.

These cookies age well when stored in an air tight container. In fact, they taste better after several days because the flavors melt together.

Yield: about 36 cookies

Originally, a chinook meant the summer wind that blew from Willapa Bay to the Willamette Valley a hundred miles east; then the term was transferred to the equatorial trade wind, whose warmth can melt a heavy snowfall between night and morning.

ANICETTI

Chef Main's friend Don Mayovsky gave her this recipe for a favorite Italian cookie.

eggs

sugar

oil

flour

baking powder

anise seed

almond extract

Oven: 375°

Beat **5 whole eggs** at medium speed till they reach a lemon color, about 5 minutes. Add **1½ c sugar.** Beat. Add **½ c oil.** Beat.

In separate bowl blend **4½ c sifted flour, 2 t baking powder, 3 T anise seed;** add all at once to egg mixture. Mix. Add **½ t almond extract.**

Pipe onto greased baking sheets two high rows* to a pan so that dough looks something like 2 french bread loaves.

Bake 20-25 minutes, until edges brown and center is firm. Slice into pieces about ½ inch wide with serrated knife.*

T I P S

Rows of dough should be about 3 inches wide and about 1½ inches high.

The slices may be laid out on a baking sheet on their sides and toasted for about 10 minutes.

Stored in an airtight container these cookies will improve with age.

These cookies are meant to be dipped in wine.

Yield: About 6 dozen

MOCHA HEART COOKIES

No cookie tray should be without these attractive and tasty cookies.

butter Oven: 375°

sugar Cream ½ **c butter** till soft. Add ¼ **c sugar**
egg gradually at low mixer speed. Cream 30
flour seconds. Add **1 egg,** room temperature.*

cocoa Add slowly **1½ c flour** that has been sifted
instant coffee together with **2 T cocoa powder.** Add
2 t instant coffee granules. Mix till blended.
Form dough into ball and chill at least 15
minutes. Roll out dough and cut into hearts.
Bake for 7 to 10 minutes.

T I P S

Run the egg, still in the shell, under warm water to bring it to room temperature.

For a special treat, dip each cookie in melted dark chocolate so that the heart is half covered.

Yield: 20 to 25 cookies

BEAVER BREAD

Every Sunday at 1:00 p.m., Faye Beaver arrives. In her nineties, Ms. Beaver remembers days on the peninsula that few others do.

She really doesn't need to order when she sits down to brunch since her menu is known to any who might serve her at table 10 where she always sits. As an honored and special guest, she is deferred to in many ways: not only do the chefs peel her strawberries so she doesn't have to deal with the annoyance of the seeds, there is Beaver tea (the chefs keep a special supply of tea for her) to accompany her Monte Cristo—a gruyere cheese, turkey, and ham sandwich dipped in egg batter, especially prepared for her by Chef Lucas. And, of course, she is served only Beaver Bread prepared for her and named for her by Chef Main.

yeast	Oven: 350°
water	Dissolve **1 cake active yeast** in
flour	**½ c warm water** (90°). Stir **2 T flour** into
milk	yeast mixture to form a sponge. Let mixture
butter	work for 10 minutes.
sugar	Bring ⅔ **c milk** to a boil. Remove from heat.
salt	Stir in **2 T butter, ⅓ c sugar, ¾ t salt.** Stir
eggs	till dissolved; cool to luke warm.
cinnamon	Into the sponge stir **2 lightly beaten eggs**
nutmeg	and the milk mixture. Add **5 c all-purpose**
mace	**flour, 1 t cinnamon, ¼ t nutmeg,**
	¼ t mace.*

Knead until smooth and place in greased bowl to rise till doubled. Punch down and shape into two loaves. Place in 2 greased pans and let rise ½ hour or till doubled.

Brush the top of each loaf with an egg wash made of **1 egg** beaten together with **1 t water.**

Bake for 30 minutes until bread is a golden brown.

T I P S

This mixture should provide a moist dough which holds its shape.

Bread does freeze. You can either freeze the dough and let it thaw in the refrigerator or freeze the baked loaves. It is preferable to freeze the dough.

This dough is used in Bear Claws, see p. 36.

Yield: 2 loaves

BRAN BREAD

The fragrance of baking bread is as much a part of a visit to the ARK as are the wonderful meals the diner enjoys. Chef Main's specialities range from several varieties of herbed French bread through delightful sweet rolls and muffins. The bakery display case entices both guests waiting to be seated and those whose smiles mean only one thing—the end of a fine meal.

It would be impossible to guess just how many people who spend a weekend on the peninsula have dinner at the ARK on Friday night and then take a loaf of bran bread or a bag of Bear Claws back to their motel or cabin "just to have something to start the day with" on Saturday morning.

water
milk
bran flakes
sugar
salt
butter
molasses
yeast
whole wheat flour
white flour
orange peel
walnuts

Oven: 375°

Bring to boil **1 c water, ¾ c milk** combined. Stir in **1 c bran flakes,* 3 T sugar, 1½ t salt, 6 T butter, ⅓ c molasses.** Cool to lukewarm.

Dissolve **2 pkg dry yeast** in **½ c warm water.**

Add bran mixture to yeast mixture. Add **3 c whole wheat flour, 2¾ c white flour, 1 t orange peel,** finely grated, **1½ c chopped walnuts.***

Place in bowl, cover with plastic wrap and let rise till doubled, about 1 to 1½ hours.

Punch down, form into 2 loaves. Place in 2 well-greased loaf pans. Let rise about 30 minutes.

Bake 30 minutes.

T I P S

Be sure to use bran flakes, not bran cereal.

Raisin fanciers may substitute 1 c raisins
for nuts.

This bread is a natural for turkey sandwiches.

Yield: 2 loaves

*almon cheeks
are a delicacy
usually unavailable
because most of the head
of the salmon is waste.
To save space and weight
in transport, the fish
heads get tossed away.
The cheeks, a bit larger
than a powder puff, have
a more delicate salmon
flavor than the fillets and
steaks most people know.*

TOMATO PESTO TWIST BREAD

Tomato Pesto Twist bread was introduced at the 1985 Garlic Festival. But it isn't just the garlic dinner that brings people to Nahcotta each June. One of the special features of the Garlic Festival each year is a walking, talking garlic. No, Nanci and Jimella have not had Tom develop some strange new hybrid at the farm, but they do honor one of the employees each year as the Garlic Princess. This princess then graces the festival dressed as a giant garlic bulb.

Several garlics from the past still maintain strong ties with the restaurant. Alise, the first garlic, is a Long Beach native and, though she's moved on to Seattle, regularly comes back to visit, often helps out with publicity, her profession now. Darcy followed her sister Alise both as a waitress at the ARK and as Garlic II. While her studies may take her off to Seattle during the winter, when she comes back to the ARK dining room, taking dinner orders and making wine recommendations, it's as though she's never been away.

Tamara, the fourth Garlic, does prep work in the kitchen where she's become an expert in all those tasks, from oyster shucking and calamari cleaning to lettuce cutting, that, though invisible, are essential to making an ARK meal so special. She'll be happy to demonstrate the fine art of lettuce drying which she does by swinging a large cloth full of washed lettuce in a clockwise arc. For right-handed lettuce swinging, she will tell you, the left foot is the forward base foot and the swinger rocks back and forth onto the right foot. Of course, for left-handed swinging, it's just the opposite.

sugar	Oven: 350°
salt	Dissolve **3 T sugar, 1 t salt, 2 c milk,**
dried milk	**2 T butter** in saucepan over medium heat.
butter	Add **2 T dried onion flakes.** Cool to
onion flakes	lukewarm.
eggs	Beat **1 egg** lightly.
yeast	Dissolve **1 cake fresh yeast** in ⅓ c water,
water	heated to 90°.
flour	Combine sugar and yeast mixtures with egg.
pesto	Add **4 c all-purpose flour**; divide dough
tomato sauce	in half.
chili powder	Add **1 T pesto*** to one half, kneading it
garlic	while adding flour to make a smooth ball.

Add to the second half **1 T tomato sauce, ½ t chili powder, ½ t minced garlic.**

Cover each ball, let rise till double, about 45 minutes to one hour. Punch down.

Form each into a long roll about 2 inches in diameter. Braid them around one another, pinching at ends.

Place on greased baking sheet. Let rise till double, about 30 minutes. Brush with egg wash (**1 egg** mixed with **1 t water**).

Bake about 25-35 minutes.

T I P S

For pesto recipe, see p. 175.

Yield: 1 loaf

ITALIAN HERB ROLLS

Getting up at 2:30 in the morning doesn't sound like much fun, but you do it because if you want to catch a chinook salmon, you have to go by their hours. The ocean is not a shopping mall that opens at 9; your boat leaves at about 3:30 AM. It's cool out there in the dark morning hours; the wind off the water can chill you some. But the boats that take people out to go fishing do have coffee pots. And hooray. Today you thought to bring along some of Chef Main's herb rolls. Just right for a cool morning. The perfect treat for a 4 AM lunch on the ocean.

yeast	Oven: 350°
sugar	Mix **2 cakes fresh yeast (4 t dry yeast),**
all purpose flour	**2 T sugar, ½ c all-purpose flour** into
water	**½ c warm water (90°)** till smooth. Cover
milk	sponge with plastic wrap. Let proof for 20
molasses	minutes.
salt	Meanwhile scald **1 c milk;** pour over
butter	**3 T molasses, 1 t salt, ¼ c soft butter,**
dried onions	**2 T dried onions, 1 clove garlic, minced.** Let sit till lukewarm.
garlic	Add **1 egg** to liquid ingredients. Then add
egg	sponge to liquid. Stir in **2 c whole wheat**
whole wheat flour	**flour, 2½ c all-purpose flour** mixed with
oregano	**1 T oregano, 1 T marjoram, 1 T sage.**
marjoram	Let rise 1 to 1½ hours or until double.
sage	Punch down, cut into 16 equal parts. Form each into a "flower roll" by rolling each section of dough into a strip about 6" or 7" long then tying the strip into a loose knot and tucking the ends under.

Let rise for ½ hour. After 15 minutes, brush tops with egg wash made of **1 egg** beaten with **1 t water.** Bake for 20 to 30 minutes. When rolls begin to brown in oven, brush again with same egg wash.

Yield: 16 rolls

From the 1920's to the early 1940's, the Heckes family ran a boarding house in the historic Crellin house at Oysterville and served, among other things, thousands of wild blackberry pies, mostly made from the berries picked by their enthusiastic guests. After a meal there Duncan Hines said it was one of the five outstanding eating places in southwest Washington.

The Chinook Indians were a friendly, peaceable tribe living around the mouth of the Columbia River and along the shores of Willapa Bay. They befriended the settlers rather than attacking them. When Indian troubles inland inspired the men of Oysterville to start building their own log fort, the Chinooks laughed so hard that the blockhouse was abandoned.

One of the tribe's most important villages was at Chinookville, very near the present-day town of Chinook, which automatically acquired the same name.

And it was only natural that the tribal name should be given to the choicest fish in the river. To those who fish, those who cook fish, and those who eat it, a chinook means the king of salmon.

NOTES

Ark Extras

BEETS, PEAS & PARSNIPS

If you're lucky enough to find yourself at the Zimmerman farm someday, Tom or his father might have a few minutes to show you the garden area which produces so many of the fine vegetables that go into an ARK meal: the lettuce, the beets, the peas, the parsnips, the spinach, the carrots. Not fifty feet from the Gray's River and no more than a quarter of a mile from the last covered bridge in the State of Washington the vegetables grow in a surprisingly sheltered valley.

Tom has lived on the farm for over 10 years, since he was a young teenager, and there's little question but that farming provides the substance of his life. It's not just a job or what he happens to do. It's his work, and his work is what he's about. He shakes his head and seems older than his years when he wonders why most of his classmates from the Naselle High School have moved away. "There's so much here." But then, Tom is not only unafraid of work, his smile warms your face, your spirit, when he describes the rich lava soil of the northwest and its potential for anyone willing to take time to nurture it.

Taking advantage of natural sources for crop enrichment is central to Tom's philosophy of farming. His bright red radishes have a particularly delicate flavor since he makes sure they get extra water to cut their bitterness. The surprising mildness of his swiss chard reflects the skills and wisdom of this young farmer who refuses the aid of synthetic fertilizers. Reaching down to pull a bright orange carrot that will soon crack sweetly between your teeth, you will see some of the small white flakes of shrimp and crab shells that dot the soil around the vegetables, the final visible remnants of the natural fertilizer from the previous spring. And do you wonder about the "weeds?" Well, Tom has surrounded the garden plot with a border of Canadian thistles because their deep tap roots carry nutrients up to the plants with shallower root systems.

MARINATED GARLIC ASPARAGUS SALAD

Try this marinade on the first asparagus of the season.

lemon
bay leaf
garlic
white peppercorns
mustard seed
salt
sugar
star anise
water
distilled vinegar
cider vinegar
asparagus
red onion

Roll **one lemon*** and squeeze juice into pot. Drop in rind. Add **3 bay leaves, 6 cloves peeled garlic, 1 T white peppercorns, 1 T mustard seed, 2 T salt, 3 T sugar, 6 whole anise stars, 2 c water, 3 c distilled vinegar, 1 c cider vinegar.** Boil for 10 minutes; let stand for 15 minutes.

Wash and layer in a large bowl or crock **2 to 3 lbs trimmed asparagus** and **2 to 3 medium sized thinly sliced red onions.*** Pour brine over while still hot. Set aside for 24 to 48 hours.

T I P S

Rolling a lemon before cutting causes the fruit to release more juice when squeezed.

Slice the onions thin, but leave them in whole rounds.

Serve with wedge of tomato, add peeled, seeded cucumber on a bed of salad greens.

Makes a wonderful part of a crudite presentation.

Serves: 8 to 10

CARROTS WITH CRANBERRIES AND HAZELNUTS

This recipe was featured in the *Chicago Tribune* as part of a 1984 all-American Thanksgiving dinner.

carrots
butter
salt
pepper
garlic
shallots
hazelnuts
brown sugar
sherry
cranberry puree
orange zest

Saute **10 cooked sliced carrots** in **4 T butter. Salt, pepper** to taste. Add **2 t minced garlic, 2 t minced shallots, ¼ c chopped hazelnuts.** After 3 to 4 minutes, add **2 T brown sugar.**

After 30 seconds deglaze with **⅓ c sherry.**

Remove to serving plate. Spoon **½ c cranberry puree*** over top and garnish with **orange zest.**

T I P S

For cranberry puree recipe, see p. 192.

Serves: 8

SAUTEED BEETS WITH APPLES

The piquancy of the raspberry vinegar and apple flavors highlights this fine handling of that old staple, the beet.

red beets
butter
apple
salt
pepper
lemon
garlic
shallots
clove
raspberry vinegar
sherry
brown sugar

Trim **4 red beets.** * Place in hot water; after it comes to boil, cook for 10 to 15 minutes, checking frequently. The centers should be firm to the touch.

Remove from heat, drain, immerse in cold water, peel and cool about 45 minutes. Then slice thinly.

Saute the beets in **½ c clarified butter** * along with **1 diced apple, salt, pepper, juice of ½ lemon, 1 t minced garlic, 1 t minced shallots, 1/8 t ground cloves.** As it heats, add **⅓ to ½ c raspberry vinegar,** * **¼ c sherry.**

When beets warm through, sprinkle with **¼ c brown sugar.** Carmelize the sauce; serve hot.

T I P S

Trim at base of stem. Do not cut into beet.

For clarified butter technique, see p. 34.

For raspberry vinegar recipe, see p. 193.

Serves: 6 to 8

LEMON-SOY CARROTS

Across the country college students look for summer work every year; Kendall and Teresa know where they'll be when summer comes: back at the ARK. Kendall didn't know until a year ago what she would major in: Math or Music. (She is an accomplished viola player.) Now she plans to major in Psychology. She began at the ARK as a bus person, shy, uncertain, soft spoken. Now she moves with confidence, no longer an adolescent, rather an accomplished professional waitress. Teresa, an electrical engineering major at Seattle University, did not start as a bus person; her roots are in the kitchen. She has cut, ground, cleaned, scrubbed, chopped, floured (lightly), shucked, sliced. She has washed dishes, floors, scoured walls. And everything she does, she does enthusiastically. When she is in the kitchen, it takes on a new vitality. She, like a good many others, has spent part of her growing up at the ARK.

carrots	Peel and slice into rounds **4 carrots.**
soy sauce	Parboil for 2 to 3 minutes. Immerse in cold
lemon	water. Drain.
garlic	Combine **¾ c soy sauce, juice of 4**
olive oil	**lemons, 1 T minced garlic, 2 T olive oil.**
	Pour sauce over carrots and refrigerate in large covered container.*

T I P S

These carrots will keep for 10 to 14 days.

These carrots with their extra tang make a great side dish or a fine garnish for a garden salad.

Bay and Ocean

FENNEL POTATOES

Brunch at the ARK isn't complete without the fennel potatoes that Chef Lucas uses to accompany so many of the fine Sunday special entrees. People accustomed to more traditional potato-vegetable combinations will be delighted by the extra zip provided by the addition of fennel.

red potatoes	Oven: 375°
celery	Wash, boil **8 medium sized red potatoes**
onion	until tender to the fork. Slice, lay in baking
bell pepper	pan. Add **3 ribs finely chopped celery,**
salt	**1 finely diced medium sized white**
pepper	**onion, 1 chopped bell pepper. Salt,**
butter	**pepper to taste.** Drizzle **6 T clarified**
fennel	**butter*** over vegetables. Sprinkle with **1 T**
parmesan cheese	**fennel,** mortared or run through food
sherry	processor or blender, and **parmesan cheese.**
	Pour **1 c sherry** in bottom of pan.

Bake for 25 to 30 minutes.

T I P S

For clarified butter technique, see p. 34.

Serves: 6 to 8

BADER'S PARSNIPS

Chef Lucas developed this recipe for parsnips with her friend Emily Bader, so she named the dish after her.

parsnips
sesame oil
garlic
ginger
salt
white pepper
lemon
rice vinegar
sherry
brown sugar
parsley
orange zest

Peel and slice into rounds or julienne **3 to 4 parsnips.** Parboil to crisp yet tender. Drain. Immerse in ice and and cold water.

Place **6 T sesame oil** in saute pan. Add parsnips, **1 t minced garlic, 1 t minced fresh ginger, salt and white pepper** to taste, **juice of one lemon, ⅓ c rice vinegar.**

Saute until vegetables are hot. Deglaze with **¼ c sherry.**

Add **3 T brown sugar** and heat until sauce is carmelized (thick and brown).

Deglaze again with **¼ c sherry.** Cook till sauce re-carmelizes.

Top with **chopped parsley** and **orange zest** before serving.

Serves: 2

GARLIC SZECHWAN

This combination of garlic, teriyaki sauce, and szechwan peppers is not for the faint of heart, but it is delicious. The heavy flavor may overpower some more subtly flavored dishes, but a garlic fan would be making a serious mistake by missing Garlic Szechwan.

garlic
dry vermouth
olive oil
butter
sesame oil
ginger
szechwan pepper
sake
teriyaki

Oven: 225°

Peel excess skin from **2 heads garlic.** * Put in baking dish with **1 c dry vermouth, 3 T olive oil.** Bake 30 minutes. Baste. Cover tightly; bake for 1 hour.*

Remove cloves from skin.* Set aside. Heat **1 T clarified butter,** * **2 T sesame oil.** Add **garlic cloves, ⅓ T freshly ground ginger, szechwan pepper** and deglaze with **¼ c sake.** Add **½ c teriyaki sauce.** * Reduce till carmelized.

T I P S

Do not expose cloves; trim only excess skin.

Do not overcook: garlic is done when brown, soft, firm.

Garlic cloves will pop from skins when gently squeezed.

For clarified butter technique, see p. 34.

For teriyaki sauce recipe, see p. 174.

Serve with french bread, chevre, sliced cucumbers and a hearty red wine—merlot, pinot noir, beaujolais—or a fruity/oaky chardonnay.

Serves: 4

CHANTERELLES WITH HAZELNUTS AND MADEIRA

Once you've eaten chanterelles, you'll have trouble substituting. But since the season is short and these very special mushrooms aren't available everywhere, you can substitute small button mushrooms. Chef Lucas says that, while it won't be the same, it will certainly be a treat.

butter
salt
white pepper
tabasco
worcestershire sauce
shallots
garlic
hazelnuts
paprika
chanterelles
madeira
parsley

Place in a sauce pan **4 to 6 T clarified butter,* salt and white pepper** to taste, **1 dash tabasco, 1 t worcestershire sauce, ½ t shallots,** minced, **1 t garlic,** minced, **2 T hazelnuts,** coarsely ground, **1/8 t paprika,** and **2 c chanterelles,** wiped and cut in half. Turn heat on to high.

As the toasting aroma of nuts and garlic rises, deglaze with **½ c madeira.** Cook just long enough to reduce sauce slightly. Serve in casserole or chafing dish. Sprinkle with chopped **parsley.**

T I P S

For clarified butter technique, see p. 34.
Serves: 4

OYSTERS WITH ARTICHOKE HEARTS

Served on the half shell, these oysters make an elegant first course that is similar to traditional oysters au gratin. The ARK touch, however, turns them into something truly special.

oysters
flour
butter
mushrooms
shallots
garlic
parsley
tabasco
lemon
artichoke heart
dijon mustard
rock salt
brandy
fish stock
heavy cream
parmesan
chives

Dust lightly **6 to 8 extra small oysters*** in **flour.** Pan fry* in **4 T clarified butter*** in a very hot skillet until slightly crisp on one side.

Turn oysters and add **⅓ c mushrooms,** sliced, **1 t shallots, 1 t garlic,** minced, a **sprinkle of chopped parsley,** a **dash tabasco, squeeze of lemon, 1 artichoke heart,** diced,* **½ t dijon mustard.*** Remove oysters and place in half shell on **rock salt** in oven dish.

Deglaze with **2 or 3 T brandy,** add **2 T fish stock,* ⅓ c heavy cream.** Reduce sauce and lace over oysters. Sprinkle loosely shredded **parmesan** over oysters and finish under broiler for several minutes.

Garnish with **2 T chives,** sliced, or spring onion ends.*

T I P S

You can triple the recipe, but don't try to cook more than 6 to 8 oysters at once or you'll have an oyster massacre. If you want to do more, pan fry them to a perfect brown, remove to a casserole, and add the sauce later.

Use a 10" to 12" saute skillet.

For clarified butter technique, see p. 34.

Cut artichoke in a small dice so that it doesn't overwhelm the oyster in the shell.

Before removing oysters be sure dijon is thoroughly incorporated into sauce.

For fish stock recipe, see p. 194.

For an alternate presentation, top the oysters with Italian Bread Crumbs (see p. 31) and slip them under the broiler or in a 450° oven just long enough to brown crumbs.

Serves: 2 as an appetizer

GARLIC STUFFED MUSHROOMS

This appetizer recipe is a good foundation recipe: it can be varied easily to achieve new presentations. For example, try adding a little shrimp, crab or artichoke hearts, finely diced. Or read over the ingredients and decide what your variation will be. Then do it.

mushrooms
butter
garlic
hazelnuts
pernod
bread crumbs
parsley
paprika
parmesan
salt
black pepper
dry vermouth

Oven: 350°

Stem and brush or wipe **18 to 20 mushrooms,** chop stems fine and saute in **3 to 4 T clarified butter.*** Add **4 to 5 minced cloves garlic, ⅓ c finely chopped hazelnuts.**

When mushroom stems lose their liquid, deglaze with **⅓ c pernod.** Add mixture to **1½ c bread crumbs.** Add **2 T chopped parsley, 1/8 t paprika, ½ c parmesan.** Add **salt, pepper** to taste. Set aside.

Wipe inside of each cap with **melted or clarified butter.*** Fill cavity with stuffing; top with **grated parmesan.** Put stuffed mushrooms in baking dish and drizzle **melted or clarified butter** over tops. Add **dry vermouth** to bottom of dish.

Bake 15-20 minutes till cheese is melted and lightly browned.

T I P S

For clarified butter technique, see p. 34.

Do not overbake; mushrooms should not get mushy—they should be firm when served.

Serves: 5 to 6

POTATO-LEEK SOUP

Kathy Lattin, a friend of the Ark Chefs, provided this Potato-Leek Soup recipe. This soup can be used as the first course in a meal or accompanied by a basket of brioche or a loaf of Tomato Pesto Twist Bread for lunch.

leeks

butter

garlic

potatoes

vegetable bouillon

water

peas

watercress

sour cream

salt

white pepper

Trim root ends and tough leaves from **2 bunches (6 to 8) leeks.** Wash well. Cut in ½" pieces lengthwise. Rinse well and slice thin.

Melt **5 T butter** in heavy 3 quart saucepan. Add leeks, cook till soft but not brown. Add **3 cloves garlic,** chopped. Add **3 medium potatoes,** chopped. Add broth of **3 cubes vegetable bouillon** dissolved in **4 c water.** Bring to boil. Reduce heat. Simmer gently uncovered for 20 minutes.

Add **1 c fresh peas.** Cook 5 minutes. Add **1 bunch watercress.***

Whirl soup in blender till smooth. Return to saucepan. Add **¾ c sour cream** stirring constantly.* Add **salt** and **white pepper** to taste.

Garnish with dollop of sour cream and sprig of watercress.

T I P S

If watercress is unavailable, substitute parsley.

Sour cream burns and sticks to the pan almost immediately so stirring is quite important.

Serves: 6 to 8

GARLIC ORANGE BISQUE

This soup made its debut at the 1984 Garlic Festival at the ARK.

butter

olive oil

carrots

garlic

jalapenos

walnuts

oranges

orange juice concentrate

sherry

garlic stock

roux

heavy cream

avocado

Melt **3 T butter** and **3 T olive oil** in saute pan. Add **2 small carrots,** * finely chopped, **4 T garlic,** minced, **3 to 4 jalapenos,** seeded and finely chopped, **1 c walnuts,** finely chopped. Cook over medium heat for 10 to 15 minutes, until slightly caramelized.

Chop fine **3 whole oranges,** skin included, in food processor. Add to carrot mixture, stir until well-blended. Add **6 oz orange juice concentrate.** Continue sauteing for a minute or two. Put mixture in stockpot. Deglaze saute pan with **½ c sherry.** Add to stockpot.

Add **1½ qts garlic stock,** * bring to low boil. Simmer 15 minutes. Pour through sieve, discard pulp.

Add **1 c roux,** * stirring constantly. Add **2 to 3 c heavy cream,** whisking slowly, to thin and blend the soup into a smooth cream texture. Heat slowly, but do not boil.

Serve topped with dollop of sour cream, 2 small slices of **ripe avocado.**

T I P S

Carrots, garlic and jalapenos can be chopped together in food processor. Process walnuts separately.

For garlic stock recipe, see p. 196.

For roux recipe, see p. 34.

Yield: 1½ quarts

GARLIC ROSE SOUP

Diners who were lucky enough to get reservations for the Garlic Festival Dinner in 1983 found themselves feasting on a meal in which every course featured garlic. This Garlic Rose Soup set the tone for a lovely meal.

garlic
shallots
butter
flour
tomatoes
parsley
sherry
garlic stock
rose water
salt
pepper
whipping cream
creme fraiche
candied rose petals

Saute **14 minced cloves garlic, 4 minced shallots** in **3 T clarified butter.*** When garlic begins to turn brown, add **2 T flour.** Stir 1 to 2 minutes. Add **6 to 8 small diced tomatoes, 2 T chopped parsley, 1 c sherry, 7 c garlic stock,* 2 dashes rose water, salt, pepper to taste.** Bring to near boiling, simmer about 10 minutes. Finish with **2 c whipping cream.**

Garnish with dollops of **creme fraiche*** top each serving with **candied rose petals.***

T I P S

For clarified butter technique, see p. 34.

For garlic stock recipe, see p. 196.

For creme fraiche recipe, see p. 35.

For candied rose petal technique, see p. 35.

Serves: 8 to 10

Dinner at the Ark

Sounds From The Kitchen

Fire a feed.
2 Kasseris.
Out on 4.
I need a sub.
Behind.
Could you do a Garlic Szechwan for table 14?
They've been here four nights in a row.
A gas burner roars onto high.
The dishwasher rumbles.
I'm behind you.
Silverware slurps into the soaking pan.
1 f&c for the bar.
Can you take this dijonnaise?
Bread for 3.
Plates clatter.
Bread for 9.
Bread for 4.
Lot of babies out there; we're out of high chairs.
Anne and her mother and sister are on 21.
I need the cranberry-grand marnier sauce.
No more trifles.
I need a follow-up on 6, please.
Behind.
A Greek-style Prawns flames up as Jimella pours a
round of ouzo into the saute pan.
Table 16 says they've never had better salmon.
Where's that special ap?
Tell them thank you.
Oven's down.
The door to the walk-in thuds shut.
It's all been walk-ins since 8:30.
Out on 7.
There's a great sunset out back.
Behind, I'm behind you.
A saute pan clatters to the back burner where the
dishwasher will pick it up.
The oil sizzles in the deep fryer as Cheryl lowers a
fish and chip order.
Off on 21.
And always, always the clatter-music of silverware
and glasses...

HALIBUT WITH CRANBERRY PORT SAUCE

The rich rosy color of the cranberry port sauce is the first clue to how good this dish will be.

flour
halibut
butter
garlic
shallots
lemon
port
madeira
cranberry puree
fish stock
cream
orange zest

For each serving saute a **lightly floured* 6 oz halibut fillet** in **2 T clarified butter.*** Add **1 t minced garlic, 1 t minced shallot, juice of a lemon wedge.**

Deglaze with **⅓ to ½ c port,* ¼ c madeira.**

Add **¼ c cranberry puree.*** Pour on **¼ c fish stock*** and **2 to 3 T heavy cream.**

When halibut is done,* remove.

Reduce stock; pour over halibut.

Garnish halibut with **orange zest.**

T I P S

Be sure to shake off excess flour to prevent burning.

For clarified butter technique, see p. 34.

Use a sweet dessert wine; Ficklin makes a very good one.

For cranberry puree recipe, see p. 192.

For fish stock recipe, see p. 194. Fish bouillon may be substituted.

Be sure not to overcook halibut. Poke flesh or fish with finger: springiness means doneness.

Recipe is per serving; multiply as needed.

HALIBUT WITH RED PEPPER SAUCE

In addition to the regular menu, Chef Lucas features one or two special entrees and a special appetizer each evening. Her Halibut with Red Pepper Sauce appears occasionally on the Specials Board and always draws a number of questions—and, once the presentation is explained, many orders. Halibut can stand up to the full flavor of the Red Pepper Sauce and anyone who has made this selection leaves the restaurant with that special ARK smile of satisfaction

To create the ARK feeling anywhere, try this entree accompanied by rice pilaf and then close your eyes and listen for the sound of the tide flowing into the bay outside your window.

halibut
butter
lemon
salt
pepper
sherry
red pepper sauce

Fry **2 halibut fillets, 6 oz each,** in **4 T clarified butter.** * Brown lightly on one side; turn, add **juice of ¼ lemon, salt, pepper** to taste. Pour **¼ c sherry** around the edges. Serve laced with **2 to 3 T red pepper sauce.** *

T I P S

For clarified butter technique, see p. 34.

For red pepper sauce, see p. 170.

Ling cod may be substituted for halibut.

Serves: 2

SALMON WITH WILD BLACKBERRY PRALINE SAUCE

Set your alarm for 3 A.M. and sleep fitfully because you know that you're going to oversleep and your salmon charter will leave without you. Wake groggily and dress in four layers of clothes you had to borrow because you never dreamed your week at the beach would include anything like a pre-dawn fishing trip and anyway it would never have occurred to you to pack a rain poncho and wool gloves for a July vacation. Grumble at the friends who told you this would be fun even though everybody knows you need 7 hours of sleep. Fill your thermos with coffee, and throw it in the back of the car. Then worry that you didn't screw the lid on tight.

You're on your way to your first fishing trip, and you're leaving Ilwaco Boat Basin at 4 A.M. Out through Baker Bay and across the bar from the Columbia River into the Pacific Ocean. Should you have taken dramamine? It's still dark when you leave, but the boat you're on seems to be part of a small armada going out into the dark ocean. You and several of the charterers huddle in the cabin while two brave souls stand out in the wind and watch the captain and his helper get ready for the day of fishing. Finally at a spot that's supposed to be good, you all get your rods and lines and then wait. "What happens if something happens?" you ask and then realize how little you know about what you're doing.

Several hours later, you've retreated to the cabin and some coffee, wondering how long this ordeal will last. No one on the boat has caught a salmon except the guy who does it every day. One of your friends is sick, and it's not even 7 A.M. yet. You start to drift to sleep clutching your soothing hot drink when someone shakes your shoulder lightly. "You've got one."

"Huh?" you ask.

"Come on, you've got one."

You stumble out to your station on the deck and sure enough, something is tugging at your line.

"What now?" you ask vacantly.

"Reel it in, of course."

Intimidated by the apparent competence around you, you do as told and reel in a chinook salmon, a fifteen pounder. Suddenly the boat doesn't rock as much, you're wide awake, the air warms as the sun breaks through, and you wonder why you haven't gone fishing before. This has to become a regular part of any vacation, every year.

salmon fillet
flour
butter
shallot
garlic
lemon
dijon mustard
raspberry vinegar
madeira
blackberry puree
fish stock
heavy cream
garlic almond pralines

For each serving pan fry **1 salmon fillet, 4 to 6 oz,** dusted with **flour,*** in ¼ c **clarified butter.*** Add **1 minced shallot, 1 minced garlic clove,** juice of **1 wedge of lemon, ½ t dijon mustard, 1 T raspberry vinegar.***

Deglaze with ⅓ c **madeira.** Add **2 to 3 T blackberry puree,*** ¼ c **fish stock.*** Reduce. Add **2 to 3 T heavy cream.** Top with **garlic almond pralines.***

(continued)

T I P S

Be sure to shake off excess flour to prevent burning.

For clarified butter technique, see p. 34.

For raspberry vinegar, see berry vinegar recipe p. 193.

For blackberry puree, see raspberry puree recipe p. 191.

For fish stock recipe, see p. 194. Fish bouillon may be substituted.

For garlic almond pralines, see p. 189.

Recipe is per serving; multiply as needed.

*N*orthwest Indians **prepared something that became known as squaw candy by cutting strips from both the sides and belly of a salmon such as the low fat chum, then salt-brining and hot-smoking them.**

SALMON WITH WILD HUCKLEBERRY SAUCE

A particularly good year for the tiny, tangy wild red huckleberries from the Northwest inspired Chef Lucas to create this entree. Unfortunately, these berries are not available in many parts of the country, and even in the Northwest the season is short. Chef Lucas encourages people to try the recipe with blueberries.

salmon
flour
butter
lemon
salt
white pepper
garlic
shallots
madeira
huckleberry puree
heavy cream
hazelnuts
huckleberries

For each serving, dust **1 fillet of fresh salmon, 6 oz,** with **flour.** * Brown slightly on one side in **3 T clarified butter** * heated in a skillet. Add **juice from 1 lemon wedge, salt** and **white pepper** to taste.

Turn salmon, adding **1 t minced garlic, 1 t minced shallots.** Brown second side gently. Deglaze pan with **3 T madeira.** Add **3 T huckleberry puree,** * ¼ c heavy cream.** Marry cream and puree by moving pan in circular motion.

Remove to serving dish and pour sauce over salmon. Sprinkle with toasted **hazelnuts** and fresh **huckleberries.**

T I P S

Be sure to shake off excess flour to prevent burning.

For clarified butter technique, see p. 34.

For huckleberry puree, cook together 1 c fresh or frozen huckleberries, 1 t granulated sugar, squeeze of juice from ½ lemon, ¾ c merlot. When berry skins pop, puree well in blender or food processor and pass mixture through sieve.

Recipe is per serving; multiply as needed.

BLACKENED SALMON A LA ARK

Chef Lucas has responded to the interest in Cajun cooking that has spread throughout the country in the past few years with her own version of blackened fish. Using the Northwest salmon, she has developed a dish that combines the best of two regions.

salmon fillets
butter
almonds
parsley
granulated garlic
paprika
chili powder
thyme
curry powder
dill
sherry
lemon

Coat **4 salmon fillets, 6 to 7 oz each,** with **6 T clarified butter,*** making sure both sides of each fillet are well covered. Remove to dry plate. Sprinkle generously with mixture* of **5 T finely chopped almonds, 2 T finely chopped parsley*, 1½ T granulated garlic, 1 T paprika, 2 T chili powder, 2 T whole thyme, 1½ T curry powder, 2 T dill weed.** Pat the mixture firmly onto both sides of each fillet.

Heat **6 to 8 T clarified butter** in skillet on medium high. When butter is hot add fillets. Cook about 4 minutes on first side, watching flesh turn pink. Turn each fillet with a fork, gently, and cook another 4 minutes.* Deglaze pan with ¼ **c dry sherry** and add **juice of 1 lemon.***

T I P S

▼

For clarified butter technique, see p. 34.

The mixture should be re-tossed just before using if it has been left to sit before using.

After chopping parsley, put it into heavy cheesecloth and wring out all the liquid. It must be dry so as not to cake the mixture.

Test for doneness by pressing the thickest part of the fillet with your finger. The firmer the fish, the more done. The flesh should have a bounce to it when touched.

To get the most juice from the lemon, roll it hard on the table before cutting.

Serves: 4

SALMON WITH HAZELNUT SAUCE

Trolling and gill-netting are the major methods of salmon fishing. In gill-netting, a net is dropped into the water and then pulled in, with any luck, full of fish. The gill-net, which may be as big as 75' x 200', is usually made of nylon and costs about $5000. One person can handle a boat and a gill-net if the boat is equipped with hydraulic, but typically two people will work together on each boat. In both gill-netting and trolling, the boats stay out from 3 to 5 days but occasionally for as long as ten days. The success of the fishing will, to some extent, determine the length of the stay since it is the storage capacity of the boat both for fuel, supplies, and for the catch, that finally limits how long a boat can stay out.

Trolling involves putting out a number of lines from the boat. Each line has a series of lines that drag out behind it with a space of about seven feet between each of these secondary lines. These troll lines might go 100 feet deep and be dragged through the water at a speed of five knots for up to four hours at a time. Many people prefer salmon caught by this method because the salmon are caught separately while the gill-net method will haul in as much as 300 pounds of fish in each drift of over an hour, often bruising their flesh.

But rest assured that no fish will ever taste like the one you catch, and no fish you ever catch will ever taste like your first Chinook.

flour	Brown both sides of **4 lightly floured***
salmon fillets	**salmon fillets, 5 oz each,** in ⅓ **c clarified**
butter	**butter.*** Add **salt, white pepper** to taste.
salt	When browned on both sides, add **1 t**
white pepper	**minced garlic, 1 t minced shallots,**
garlic	⅓ **c ground roasted filberts, juice of**
shallots	½ **lemon.**
roasted filberts	
lemon	

madeira
fish stock
dijon mustard
heavy cream
frangelico
parsley

Deglaze with ⅓ **c madeira,** add ½ **c fish stock,*** ½ **t dijon mustard.** When salmon is done, remove to warm plate.

Add ¾ **c heavy cream** to sauce in pan, reduce. Add **2 t frangelico,** let marry for about 30 seconds. Lace over fillets, sprinkle with **chopped parsley.**

T I P S

Be sure to shake off excess flour to prevent burning.

For clarified butter technique, see p. 34.

For fish stock recipe, see p. 194. Fish bouillon may be substituted.

Serves: 4

PERCH WITH PERNOD

If you haven't discovered the possibilities of Pernod in preparing fish, start with this recipe.

butter
perch
flour
egg
milk
garlic
shallots
salt
white pepper
lemon
parsley
pernod
fish stock
cream

For each serving bring **clarified butter*** to high heat. Dip **1 perch fillet, 8 to 10 oz,** in **flour,* egg wash** made of **2 beaten eggs** and **1 c milk,** then again in **flour.*** Place in hot butter; brown both sides.

Add **pinch minced garlic, pinch minced shallots, salt, pepper** to taste, **juice of 1 lemon wedge, pinch chopped parsley.**

Deglaze with **¼ c pernod.** Add **3 T fish stock.*** When fish is done,* remove to a warm plate. Reduce sauce, adding **2 to 3 T heavy cream;** let marry to a medium consistency. Lace sauce over fillet; garnish with **chopped fresh parsley.**

T I P S

For clarified butter technique, see p. 34.

Be sure to shake off excess flour to prevent burning.

For fish stock recipe, see p. 194. Fish bouillon may be substituted.

Do not overcook; fish should give some to the press of your finger.

Recipe is per serving; multiply as needed.

STURGEON SZECHWAN

There was a brief period in England when King Edward II declared the sturgeon a "royal fish" and a law required that any of the fish caught must be offered to the king. Sturgeon Szechwan lets the modern diner know just what that term "royal fish" means.

sesame oil
butter
flour
sturgeon fillets
garlic
ginger
szechwan pepper
lemon
sake
teriyaki sauce
peanuts

Heat **1½ T sesame oil** and **4 T clarified butter*** until hot. Dust lightly with **flour* 4 fillets of white sturgeon, 6 oz each,** (skin off). Pan fry until light brown on both sides. Add **½ t minced garlic, ½ t minced ginger, 2 szechwan red peppers,** diced with seeds. Cook until garlic begins to brown.

Squeeze juice from **½ lemon** over sturgeon and deglaze with **⅓ c sake.**

Add **8 T teriyaki sauce*** and reduce till carmelized.* Garnish with **chopped peanuts.**

T I P S

For clarified butter technique, see p. 34.

Be sure to shake off excess flour to prevent burning.

For teriyaki sauce recipe, see p. 174.

If sauce appears to break as it reduces, add tablespoonful of sake or sherry.

To prepare salmon szechwan, follow recipe through reduction of teriyaki sauce. Then add 1/8 c fresh peas, 1/8 c diced fresh tomatoes. Remove from heat, garnish with sprinkle of roll-cut green onions.

Serves: 4

OYSTERS A LA KEMMER

Brian Kemmer farms oysters in Willapa Bay as have members of his family for many years. He gave Chef Lucas this recipe from the old Oysterville Hotel which was operated by the Heckes family, some of his ancestors. The hotel has been gone for over fifty years, but this recipe, served then as a first course and recommended at The ARK as an entree also, preserves some of the connections with the peninsula's past which are so much a part of the restaurant.

oysters	Oven: 450°
shallots	Shuck **12 extra small oysters** and remove
sherry	muscles.*
bacon	Into a half shell for each of the oysters, place
barbeque sauce	**½ t minced shallots,** one oyster, **light lace**
extra sharp	**of sherry** to glaze oyster, **sprinkle of**
cheddar	**bacon bits** made of pre-cooked, but not
rock salt	crisp, thinly sliced bacon. Top with
	barbeque sauce* and **sprinkle of**
	shredded extra sharp cheddar.

Arrange the oyster shells on rock salt in a baking dish. Bake for 10 to 12 minutes.

T I P S

For oyster shucking, see p. 30.

The chefs suggest the barbeque sauce from their first cookbook, *The Ark: Cuisine of the Pacific Northwest,* but your favorite sauce will do.

Serves: 2 as an appetizer, 1 as an entree.

rivately owned oyster beds mean that you can find oyster share-croppers on Willapa Bay, people who farm oysters on someone else's land and split the profits with the owner. This is rather hard to visualize when the tide is in and you can't even see the oyster lines, but becomes more understandable at low tide when the bed areas look a little more like land.

SCALLOPS BAKED WITH CREAM AND PECANS

Many nights when you come to the ARK, you will have a chance to visit the lounge. Ask for a Peach Delight. Go ahead. Jan, the bartender, will be delighted. She incorporates the ARK enthusiasm for invention into her own work, taking advantage of regional and seasonal fruit to create specialty drinks both with and without alcohol to please the diners as they look over their menus. Jan moved to Seaview about five years ago, but she'd been coming to the peninsula since she was four. She remembers pestering her father regularly, "When are we going to move to the beach?" Finally, she had to grow up and do it on her own. Now she lives in a house with a second floor baclony that lets her look at the ocean and works behind the bar at the ARK where the wide windows let her look out at the bay—that is when she's not concocting some new drink to feature. Her Peach Delight is a summer favorite. And on a holiday you may very well find yourself enjoying a Midori Leprechaun for St. Patrick's Day or a bright red Raspberry Daquiri on the Fourth of July.

And if scallops baked with cream and pecans is on the menu, Jan will be happy to recommend a drink for you to sit and sip while you wait for this fine entree.

scallops	Oven: 425°
fish stock	Submerge **1½ lb fresh scallops** for 3 to 5
mushrooms	minutes* in boiling **fish stock.***
pecans	Mix together, in a large mixing bowl, scallops,
parmesan	**1 c thinly sliced mushrooms,**
lemons	**½ c coarsely chopped pecans,**
salt	**½ c grated parmesan cheese, juice of**
white pepper	**2 lemons, salt** and **white pepper** to taste.
cream	Whip **3 c whipping cream.** Fold* in
gruyere	**1 c shredded Gruyere, 1 t dijon**
dijon mustard	**mustard,** pinch of salt and **4 to 5 gratings**
	of fresh nutmeg,* **3 dashes tabasco,**
	½ c sour cream.

nutmeg
tabasco
sour cream

Place the scallop mixture into casserole and top with enough of the cream mixture to cover amply. Grate **fresh nutmeg** into center. Bake 7 to 9 minutes.

T I P S

Be very careful to avoid overcooking scallops. Remove and drain and set aside. Using a basket allows you to remove the scallops quickly from the poaching liquid.

For fish stock recipe, see p. 194.

It's important to fold: whipping these ingredients into the cream will cause the sauce to break down.

If you don't have fresh nutmeg, use 1/8 t ground nutmeg.

This dish is a perfect example of working with two different delicacies; it's critical your hand and timing should be in tune with the combination. You can break the sauce and lose your presentation, or worse yet, overcook the succulent scallop. So be aware.

You can prepare oysters with this sauce, too. If you have fresh oysters, put 1/8 t brandy in each shell. Replace oyster in shell. Place 1 T cream and pecan sauce in dollop on top of oyster. Sprinkle with grated parmesan. Bake for 4 to 5 minutes at 450°.

Serves: 4

SAUTEED SCALLOPS WITH SMOKED OYSTER SAUCE

Oysters put the Long Beach Peninsula on the map during the days of the California Gold Rush and even today oyster farming is a major industry in Willapa Bay. A visitor to the ARK must drive past a huge pile of oyster shells in order to pull into the restaurant parking lot and once seated for a meal can look out the windows to see oyster canneries and oyster beds. It's no wonder that these local delicacies spark Chef Lucas's creativity.

scallops
flour
butter
smoked oysters
mushrooms
garlic
shallots
salt
white pepper
tabasco
dijon mustard
tarragon
lemon
brandy
fish stock
cream
green onions

For each serving, dredge **5 to 6 scallops*** in **flour.** Place in skillet with **4 T clarified butter*** already hot. Add **6 petite smoked oysters,*** cut in half.

Then, add* **⅓ c sliced mushrooms, ½ t minced garlic, ½ t minced shallots, salt** and **white pepper** to taste, **2 dashes tabasco,* ½ t dijon mustard, generous pinch dried tarragon, juice of 1 wedge of lemon.** Mix ingredients.

Deglaze with **¼ c brandy.**

Add **3 T fish stock,* 3 T heavy cream.** Reduce 1 to 2 minutes until sauce thickens. Add **2 T sliced green onions.** Serve.

T I P S

Bay scallops are too small for this dish; sea scallops are better.

Cook no more than three servings per pan at a time.

For clarified butter technique, see p. 34.

Be sure to add these ingredients quickly since the scallops overcook easily.

Be sure to place the tabasco into the butter, not on any particular ingredient.

For fish stock recipe, see p. 194. Fish bouillon can be substituted.

Recipe is per serving; multiply as needed.

Oysters need cold water for their growth; they spawn during the summer when the water warms up.

SCALLOPS WITH GINGER

Driving to the ARK along Pacific Highway on the Long Beach Peninsula offers the vacationer a momentary glance at a remnant of the U.S. Life Saving Service. At Klipsan Beach, between the highway and the ocean stands the old Klipsan life-saving station. Halfway between the mouth of the Columbia River and the entrance to Willapa Bay, the site was selected because of the great number of shipwrecks along Long Beach.

From 1891, when it was established, through 1915, when the Life Saving Service became part of the Coast Guard, until 1947, the Klipsan Beach station was an important part of the peninsula life. The old white building has been modified and is now privately owned but still stands as a reminder of older times.

scallops
butter
mushrooms
salt
pepper
fresh ginger
garlic
lemon
cognac
fish stock
cream
green onion
orange zest

For each serving, saute **5 oz scallops** in **2 T clarified butter*** with ¼ **c sliced mushrooms, salt, pepper** to taste, **1 t fresh grated ginger,* 1 t minced garlic,** juice of ¼ **lemon.**

Deglaze with **2 T cognac;** add **1 T fish stock,* 3 T heavy cream.** When sauce thickens, add **1 T chopped green onion;** serve with garnish of **orange zest.**

T I P S

For clarified butter technique, see p. 34.

Mixing 1 part chopped candied ginger with 3 parts chopped fresh ginger can make a subtle difference in the sauce; this is the way Chef Lucas prepares this dish.

For fish stock recipe, see p. 194.

Recipe is per serving; multiply as needed.

CRAB AND SHRIMP CURRY

If you have curry sauce on hand, this is a quick but elegant entree. The presentation with coconut, almonds, chutney and raisins delights your most special guests or makes an evening home alone an occasion.

crab
shrimp
curry sauce
coconut
almonds
chutney
raisins

Oven: 375°

For each serving, place ¼ **to ⅓ c cooked crab meat,*** the same amount cooked cleaned **shrimp** in a baking dish. Pour **curry sauce*** over to cover. Bake 10 minutes. Sprinkle **shredded coconut** over the top and **slivered roasted almonds** around the side. Serve with **1 T chutney** and **1 T raisins** to the side.

T I P S

Dungeness crab meat works best. Ask your fish monger to give you broken legs for this dish. Sometimes the meat will blend too much with the sauce and get lost.

For curry sauce recipe, see p. 172.

Recipe is per serving; multiply as needed.

CRAB KASSERI

On a midsummer evening when the sun doesn't set until nearly ten, or during lunch on a mild day, diners looking out over the bay often see young children who were, just a moment before, sitting a table or two away. Now they're romping outside, climbing on the beached boats. The lure of the water often draws the younger guests outdoors between courses. Soon, they are no longer running free; their parents, now finished can never resist the chance to freeze the moment forever on film. A meal at the ARK is not simply a meal; it is an event, an occasion to be remembered. More than a few children and adults have pictures of themselves in front of the two-story oyster shell pile outside the front door.

crab legs
mushrooms
green onions
sherry
kasseri cheese
elegant cheese sauce
parmesan

Oven: 425°

For each serving, spread **3½ oz crab legs*** in a casserole on bed of **½ c sliced mushrooms** sprinkled with **1 T chopped green onions,** laced with **½ to 1 t sherry** for moistening. Cover with **¼ c shredded Kasseri cheese, ¾ c elegant cheese sauce.*** Sprinkle top with loosely shredded **parmesan.** Bake 12 to 15 minutes.

T I P S

Chef Lucas recommends Dungeness crab.

For elegant cheese sauce recipe, see p. 178.

Serve this crab specialty with white rice.

Recipe is per serving; multiply as needed.

VEAL PICCATA

The ARK features veal from nearby Oregon because of the chefs' commitment to cooking with the best the region has to offer.

zucchini
flour
egg
milk
butter
olive oil
veal
salt
pepper
oregano
garlic
shallots
tomato
dry vermouth
parsley

For each serving, dip slices of **zucchini** into **flour,** dip in **egg wash** made of **3 eggs** and **1 c milk,** dip once more in **flour.*** Fry in **2 T clarified butter*** and **1 T olive oil.** Set aside.

Lightly flour* **3 to 4 oz veal** pounded. Saute in **2 T clarified butter.** Season with **salt, pepper.** Add ¼ t oregano, 1 t chopped garlic, 1 t chopped shallots, ⅓ c chopped tomato.** Remove veal.

Deglaze with **¼ c dry vermouth.** Reduce.

Alternate layers of veal and zucchini. Add sauce from pan; sprinkle with **chopped parsley.**

T I P S

Be sure to shake off excess flour to prevent burning.

For clarified butter technique, see p. 34.

Recipe is per serving; multiply as needed.

VEAL WITH CAPERS

A hundred years ago the procedure was simple: first plan a town, then build a hotel. Some were small and primitive, some supremely elegant, but every peninsula community had at least one. A lot were claimed by fire within a few years of construction, and a lot outlasted their time, finally being torn down to make room for modern buildings. Probably the most elegant was the original Breakers at Tioga, just north of Long Beach; its lavishly furnished four stories catered to the fashionable wealthy from Portland. It was rebuilt after it burned in 1905, but by 1920 the new building was derelict and abandoned, at the mercy of "beachcombers" who carried away its woodwork. Until 1930 strollers on the beach could climb through what remained of its vacant window frames and inspect what was left of the salt-damaged grand piano, too big to be carted away.

Only two of the turn-of-the-century hotels still stand. The Taylor Hotel in Ocean Park, built in 1887, is on the list of historic sites, but it no longer rents rooms. The Shelburne Hotel in Seaview, first built east of the railroad tracks in 1896, was moved across the road in 1912 and attached to a boarding house that stood there. Newly renovated and furnished with antiques, it still offers fifteen bedrooms and a restaurant, which provided the first peninsular location for Nanci and Jimella's tempting food.

flour
veal
butter
salt
pepper
mushrooms
garlic
shallots
capers

For each serving saute briefly **5 oz lightly floured* veal scallops** in **2 T hot clarified butter.*** Add **salt** and **pepper** to taste. Add **¼ to ½ c sliced mushrooms, 1 t garlic, 1 t shallots, 1 T capers, 1 t dijon mustard.** Add **juice of a lemon wedge.**

mustard
lemon
cognac
madeira
cream
scallions

Pour a round*—about **2T — cognac** and deglaze with ¼ **c madeira.** Remove veal,* add **2 T heavy cream,** reduce sauce. Just before removing the sauce, add **1 t chopped scallions.**

Pour over veal and serve.

T I P S

Be sure to shake off excess flour to prevent burning.

For clarified butter technique, see p. 34.

For a round, pour the liquor around the edge of the pan.

Veal should be served rare to medium rare.

Recipe is per serving; multiply as needed.

CHICKEN PECAN A LA ARK

Greeting folks at the door many evenings is the person responsible for the fine wine list at the ARK. Kaaren has worked her way from Pennsylvania to Nahcotta, Washington, and her role as wine steward and hostess at The ARK by way of Wisconsin and California and a stint as a high school French teacher. During her off hours she is active in little theater on the Peninsula having appeared as Bloody Mary in *South Pacific* and served as costume mistress for a number of productions.

Kaaren's membership in the Northwest Enological Society keeps her up on the latest developments on Northwest wines, her specialty, so that she can provide the ARK with the information to keep its excellent cellar well stocked with regional wines as well as imported and California wines. So when you get there and would like help deciding between the Henry Estate and the Salishan Pinot Noir or between the Shafer or Hinzerling Chardonnays, call on Kaaren for advice. But, then, even if you don't you can't lose because her wine list has no losers on it.

pecans	Mix thoroughly and put into shallow bowl
paprika	**1 c coarsely chopped pecans,**
white pepper	**1/8 t paprika, 1/8 t white pepper,**
garlic	**¼ t garlic, ½ t curry. Flour** lightly
curry	**4 boned chicken breasts, 6 to 7 oz each;**
flour	dip into egg wash made of **2 eggs** mixed
chicken	well in **1 c milk.***
egg	Place chicken breasts in chopped pecan
milk	mixture; gently pat them to coat surface on
butter	both sides.
	Put **6 T clarified butter*** in large skillet. Turn on heat. Before it gets hot, add pecan coated chicken; brown lightly on both sides.*

lemon
tabasco
madeira
chicken stock
cream
nectarine

Add **1 t minced garlic, juice of** ½ **lemon, 3 dashes tabasco.** Deglaze with ⅓ **c madeira.** Add ½ **c chicken stock.***
Reduce. Add ½ **c heavy cream.** Reduce to medium consistency.

Remove chicken to warmed serving dish; lace sauce over top. Garnish with sliced **nectarines** for contrast of flavors and complement of colors.

T I P S

Be sure to shake off excess flour to prevent burning.

For clarified butter technique, see p. 34.

Watch nuts carefully so they do not start to burn.

For chicken stock recipe, see p. 195.

Serves: 4

Bay and Ocean

CHICKEN WITH ROSEMARY MARINADE

Each summer, the ARK sponsors a Garlic Festival. The area around the restaurant is transformed into a carnival with booths, a wine garden, a stage and costumed employees celebrating the "stinking rose." Artists and craftspeople from southwest Washington and northwest Oregon bring their work to display and sell. You can find everything from wreaths of garlic to garlic-decorated mugs.

Many groups, as well as the restaurant itself, offer garlic specialties to munch on as folks walk around looking at the crafts and listening to the garlic band: garlic sausage sandwiches, oysters with garlic sauce, chocolate covered garlic cloves, Gateau Allard Northwest, espresso and cappuccino.

After watching or participating in the oyster shucking contest, the garlic cleaning contest, or the garlic costume contest, you can drift over to the wine garden and taste a selection of Northwest wines.

The day finishes off with the Garlic Dinner, a seven course garlic meal—garlic featured in each menu item, and each item a delight.

chicken	Pour over **2 chickens, 1½ lb each,** or **1 chicken, 2 lb, quartered: juice of three lemons, 4 twists black pepper, ½ c olive oil, ¼ c red wine vinegar. Salt** lightly.
lemon	
pepper	
olive oil	
red wine	Boil **2 c red wine, 2 T rosemary, 1 T shallots, 2 T minced garlic** for 3 min; cool. Pour over chicken; marinate 24 hours.
vinegar	
salt	
red wine	Heat **6 oz of clarified butter*** in a saute pan and lightly flour the chicken pieces. Pan fry the chicken until thoroughly browned.
rosemary	
shallots	
garlic	
butter	
madeira	

Keep the chicken warm in the oven while preparing a sauce of the liquid left in the saute pan and 6 oz of marinade. After the liquid has cooked down, deglaze with **3 to 4 T madeira.** Serve the chicken with the sauce poured over it.

T I P S

For clarified butter technique, see p. 34.

For an alternate cooking method, glaze the chicken with butter and broil it till almost cooked. Then place it in a baking dish in the oven and finish off by baking with a sauce of sherry, lemon, garlic and rosemary poured over the meat.

Serves: 4

*O*nce the native Willapa oysters were all but extinct in the Bay, the local oyster industry relied on Japan as a source of spat except when a variety of problems made this impossible. From 1921 until 1940, the local oysterers imported seeds for the oyster Crassostrea gigas to reseed the bay. World War II made this impossible, however, so the local oyster industry began to rely on the re-seeding of the crop from the oysters in the harvest.

Again in the early 50's though, local oystermen once again imported seed from Japan to supplement the local reseeding. But a combination of pollution in the Japanese source bays, a several year stretch of bad weather, over-use of the spawning lands and the changing relationship of the dollar to the yen made it no longer economically feasible to import seed from that country by the early 70's.

NOTES

Ark Desserts

BERRY PICKING

Northwest berry pickers share one trait: they don't tell anyone, even family, where they do their best picking. Veronica Williams, who supplies the ARK with wild blackberries, is no different. Her sister picks berries, too, but not with Veronica who keeps her picking spots secret.

Rising well before dawn, Veronica may drive sixty miles to the berry patch that she knows will be ripe and ready. Climate and terrain vary the ripening dates for the berries and she doesn't want to miss the perfect picking time at each place.

She takes no chances with brambles, snakes and mosquitos—wearing heavy boots and a fisherman's rain suit over jeans and two warm shirts. She likes a rain hat—even if it's not raining, it's often damp where she goes—and ties two picking buckets to her belt to keep her hands free for picking and balance and often carries a long stick. She remembers only one bad fall when she slipped into a gully and lost all the berries she had already picked. She carries a water bottle and packs her lunch for her daily venture into the woods.

Only once did her berry picking give her a scare: a few years ago she met a bear. Fortunately she didn't get close enough for trouble but she's not anxious to run into another. She has learned through the years how to protect herself from the everyday discomforts of her avocation and won't let something like the possibility of another bear keep her from the woods.

Veronica has lived in southwestern Washington since coming to the United States as a child from Hungary after World War II. She already had an uncle living in Seattle and one living in South Bend. "They decided we should go to South Bend because we had lived in the country before and they thought we'd be happier than in the city." Veronica has never regretted their decision. She loves her home and her berry picking and "being out in the woods by myself."

RUM RAISIN TART

Chef Main based this delightful tart on a recipe from Mary McCrank who ran a family-style restaurant in Chehallis, Washington, for 45 years. Both Main and Lucas worked at Mary McCrank's Restaurant before they opened the Shelburne Restaurant. Ms. McCrank was particularly proud of the fact that she had never served alcohol in her restaurant during all its years, but she did name her poodle Murphy after the Irish whiskey of that name. Over the years people who had come as children to the restaurant grew up and brought their children for a meal of Mary's home-style fare. This recipe, inspired by Mary's Sour Cream Raisin Pie, captures all the best of her style of cooking, enhanced by Chef Main's own special touch.

all-purpose flour
salt
baking powder
butter
sugar
eggs
vanilla
milk
cornstarch
sour cream
lemon juice
raisins
nutmeg
cinnamon
salt
dark rum
cream of tartar

Crust

Oven: 350°

Sift together **2½ c all-purpose flour, ¼ t salt, 2 t baking powder.** Cream **½ c softened butter;** slowly add **1 c sugar.**

Add **2 eggs,** one at a time, scraping sides of bowl after adding each egg. Add **½ t vanilla.** Slowly add dry ingredients with **1 T milk.** Chill for 1 hour.

Divide dough in two and put half in freezer for your next tart. Roll out on lightly floured board to a thickness of ¼ inch and place gently in greased 9 inch tart pan. Pat into place. Bake crust for about 15 minutes.

Filling

Dissolve ¼ c **cornstarch** in **1½ c sour cream, 1 T lemon juice.** Mix with **½ c softened butter, 1 c raisins, 3 egg yolks,** beaten, **1/8 t nutmeg, ¼ t cinnamon, ⅓ c sugar, pinch of salt, 1 T dark rum.**

Cook to custard-like consistency in a double boiler, stirring often. Remove from heat, let cool.

Meringue Topping

Oven: 400°

Beat **3 egg whites** at medium speed until foamy. Gradually add **1 t cream of tartar, ¼ c sugar, ½ t vanilla.** Beat for 2 minutes more at medium speed, until egg whites hold peaks, are glossy but not dry.

Spread filling in tart shell. Pipe meringue over top using star tip. Bake for 5 to 7 minutes until lightly browned.

CHOCOLATE DECADENCE

Chef Main first discovered this dessert as the title recipe in the book *Chocolate Decadence*. Veronica Di Rosa of Berkeley, California, collaborated with Janice Feuer on this salute to chocolate in recipes and drawings. They both felt at the time that the American love for chocolate was peaking. But Di Rosa admits they were wrong. She told Nanci that there's just "not an end to the love of chocolate."

Anyone who's been lucky enough to try this recipe or to taste Nanci's presentation of it at The ARK would have to agree. This is the ultimate chocolate lover's chocolate treat.

bittersweet chocolate
butter
eggs
sugar
flour
whipped cream
raspberry puree

Oven: 425°

Melt **1 lb bittersweet chocolate** with **5 oz butter.** Set aside.

Combine **4 eggs** and **1 T sugar** in mixing bowl. Put over very hot water, stirring continually till eggs turn dark yellow.* Place in mixer and mix at high speed till eggs form thick ribbon when spooned up—about 5 minutes.*

Gently fold in **1 T flour.** Mix one-third of egg mixture into chocolate. Gently fold chocolate back into remaining egg mixture.

Pour into buttered and paper-lined 10" round pan.* Bake until sides start to puff up and small cracks appear but cake still appears moist, no longer than 15 minutes.

Cool, then refrigerate.

Serve each slice topped with **whipped cream** and **raspberry puree.**

T I P S

Chef Main says the eggs should be "baby bottom warm" by this time.

Mixture will triple in volume.

If you use a 9" pan, bake for 18 minutes. If you don't have a springform pan, freeze the cake and unmold by inverting pan and running hot water over it. Cake will fall out into your hand.

To serve, cut cold, let slices return to room temperature (about 10 minutes) so that texture is velvety.

For raspberry puree see p. 191.

HAZELNUT CHEESECAKE

Hazelnuts are one of the regional products that the ARK chefs turn to regularly when creating new dishes. This crustless cheesecake flavored with Frangelico combines the richness of a traditional cheesecake with the delicacy of Frangelico liqueur and hazelnuts. It also provides a tiny glimpse of the creative energy that is the essence of the ARK. Chefs Main and Lucas are not content to serve the tried and true, even when these are dishes which have helped develop the ARK's reputation. A new season, an especially good harvest, a casual conversation, or a request for something extra special for a regular patron's birthday—any of these may spark the experimentation with flavors that results in a new ARK feature.

cream cheese	Oven: 325°
sugar	Grease 10" spring form pan. Cover outside of
flour	pan with foil.
eggs	Beat **2 lbs cream cheese** till light. Scrape
vanilla	bowl regularly to remove lumps.
Frangelico	Gradually add **1¾ c sugar** and beat well.
hazelnuts	Fold in **1 T flour.** Add **4 eggs,** one at a
sour cream	time. Mix until incorporated. Add **1 t vanilla, 1 T Frangelico.** Fold in **½ lb finely ground hazelnuts.** Pour into baking pan.

Place pan in larger pan with ½" hot water in bottom. Bake for 1¼ to 1½ hours.*

Remove from oven and water bath. Remove foil from pan.

Blend **1½ c sour cream, ¼ c sugar, 1 T Frangelico, 1 t vanilla.** Pour over top of cheesecake. Return to oven for 5 minutes.

Let cool to room temperature. Refrigerate over night.*

T I P S

Cover the cake if it browns too much.

This cake takes some time to set up properly for serving.

CHIFFON CHEESECAKE

On the office windowsill at the ARK stands a ceramic head of garlic ten inches high. Perched on one of the cloves, head thrown back in laughter sits a ceramic Nanci Main. Standing next to her, leaning against the stalk, one hand in her pocket is Jimella Lucas. Former mayor of Aurora, Colorado, member of the President's council on urban affairs, director of the Denver Ballet—Norma Olsen Walker made it for the Chefs.

Norma Walker has special connections with the ARK. She shares a Swedish heritage with Chef Main's mother. Both of her daughters have worked at the ARK. Alison, studying graphic arts at the Art Institute of Seattle, waitressed while spending summers on the peninsula. Laura, a former prima ballerina, worked as a hostess. All of them have brought a special warmth, a competent grace to the ARK.

graham crackers
sugar
nutmeg
cinnamon
mace
butter
vanilla
cream cheese
sour cream
egg yolks
lemon juice
orange peel
lemon peel
fresh orange juice

Crust

Oven: 400°

Combine **1 c graham cracker crumbs, ¼ c sugar, ¼ t nutmeg, ¼ t cinnamon, ¼ t mace.** Add ⅓ to ½ c melted butter, **1 t vanilla.** Press into a 9" spring pan. Bake for 10 minutes.

Filling

Oven: 325°

Cream **1 lb 4 oz softened cream cheese*** in mixer at high speed for 3 minutes, scrape bowl.

Add **1 c sour cream.** Mix at medium speed for 2 minutes, scrape bowl again.

At lower speed, add **¾ c sugar, 2 egg yolks.** Add **¼ c lemon juice, 1 t grated orange peel, 1 t grated lemon peel, ¼ c fresh orange juice, 2 t vanilla.**

Pour filling into prebaked crust. Bake for 30 to 45 minutes.*

All ingredients should be at room temperature.

Test for doneness by shaking the sides of the pan slightly. The filling should hold like a tight custard.

Serve each slice topped with huckleberry puree. For recipe, see p. 183.

The Chinook language had become the basis for a trade language used the length of the river long before the earliest whites arrived. When the fur traders came, French and English words were added to the jargon. Few people know the language now, but by 1860 roughly a hundred thousand people in the northwest could speak and understand Chinook. The Eels dictionary, compiled in 1894, lists over fourteen hundred words, and even more phrases.

TRIPLE CHOCOLATE CHEESE CAKE

This cake, with its three distinctly colored layers, has become a staple of the ARK dessert tray.

flour
cocoa
instant coffee granules
cinnamon
butter
sugar
eggs
cream cheese
sugar
sour cream
vanilla
unsweetened chocolate
dark creme de cocoa
milk chocolate
water
white chocolate
lemon peel

Oven: 425°

Crust

Mix **1½ c flour, 2 T cocoa, 2 t instant coffee granules, ¼ t cinnamon.** Cream together **½ c butter, ¼ c sugar.** Add **1 large egg.** Incorporate dry ingredients into butter mixture.

Grease bottom and sides of 9 inch cheesecake (springform) pan. Roll out dough to ¼ inch thick on lightly floured board. Using about ½ the dough, cut a round of dough to fit the bottom of the pan. Bake for 10 minutes.*

Roll out about ⅔ of the remaining dough into a strip two inches wide.* Press strip around inside. Be sure to seal the dough so there are no cracks.

Filling

Beat **2¼ lbs softened cream cheese** till lumps vanish. Slowly add **1 c sugar.** Mix until incorporated. Sift **1 T flour** over mixture. Add **5 eggs,** one at a time, still mixing. Add **¼ c sour cream, 1 t vanilla.** Beat until ingredients are completely mixed.

Divide filling into three equal parts in separate bowls.

Into mixture in bowl one, whisk **3 oz unsweetened chocolate,** melted, **1 T dark creme de cocoa.** Pour into crust, smoothing surface of mixture, and place in freezer for 30 minutes.

Into mixture in bowl two, whisk **3 oz milk chocolate,** melted, **1 T hot water, 2 T dark creme de cocoa.** Pour over layer one, smoothing surface of mixture, and place in freezer for 30 minutes.

Into mixture in bowl three, whisk **3 oz white chocolate,** melted, **½ t lemon peel,** grated. Pour over layer two, smoothing surface.* Bake at 425° for 15 minutes. Reduce oven temperature to 200° for 45 minutes to complete baking.*

T I P S

Pre-bake the bottom crust only. Then add the sides.

Roll out extra dough and cut into tiny hearts (about ½ inch wide). Bake on lightly greased pan 5-7 minutes. Use heart cookies to garnish cheesecake.

(continued)

It is not necessary to chill the third layer before baking.

Cake will puff up slightly at sides. Center will be firm.

Cut with dry, hot knife; wipe blade after each cut and run hot water over blade periodically to keep it hot.

Chief Nakoti, for whom the town of Nahcotta, home of the ARK, is named, was buried on the peninsula in Oysterville cemetery where even now a monument stands, marking the site.

WHITE CHOCOLATE MOUSSE

This remarkably light, rich mousse has been the choice of many ARK diners since Chef Main introduced it several years ago. And you can re-create it for a festive dinner in your own home.

white chocolate
half and half
whipping cream
egg white
cream of tartar
raspberries

Shred evenly **4 oz white chocolate.** Place in hot water bath with **2½ T half & half.** Remove before fully melted; allow remainder to melt in its own heat.

Beat **½ c whipping cream** till soft peaks form. Beat **1 egg white** till opaque and add **¼ t cream of tartar.** Beat till soft peaks form. Fold one-third of egg mixture into the chocolate. Then fold in remaining two-thirds of mixture. Fold in whipped cream.

To serve, place **raspberries** in bottom of each of 4 parfait glasses and pipe ¼ of mousse into each parfait.

Cover with plastic wrap and refrigerate for at least 3 hours.

Serves: 4

CRANBERRY GRAND MARNIER MOUSSE

Chef Main needs only to drive along the back roads of the peninsula to be inspired by the cranberry bogs dotting the area. It's not surprising then to find these bright red berries garnishing many of her desserts. Her Cranberry Grand Marnier Mousse, however, makes these traditionally autumn fruits the central flavor in a truly luscious finish to a fine meal.

cranberries
water
sugar
Grand Marnier
orange rind
orange juice
gelatin
eggs
whipping cream
vanilla

Simmer **2 c cranberries, ¾ c water, ¼ c sugar** until cranberries begin to pop open. Puree and strain. Add **4 T Grand Marnier** and **1 T finely grated orange rind.**

Reserve ½ c sauce. Add **2 T Grand Marnier** and **2 T orange juice.** Set aside.

Soak **1 T gelatin** in ¼ **c cold water** till softened.

Warm **3 egg yolks** then beat with ½ **c sugar** until light and lemon colored.

Transfer to large bowl. Fold in cranberry puree.

Beat **1 c whipping cream** with ½ **t vanilla** till firm peaks form.

Beat **whites of 3 eggs** till firm.

Stir gelatin and cranberry sauce into egg yolk mixture. Fold in egg whites, ⅓ at a time. Fold in whipped cream.

To prepare individual parfaits, whip **1 c whipping cream** with **2 T Grand Marnier.** Pipe mousse into bottom of parfait glass, drizzle reserved cranberry sauce over mousse so that it reaches sides of glasses and then pipe whipping cream-Grand Marnier mixture over sauce. Repeat these steps so that there are six layers in each glass.

T I P S

Top with whipped cream rosette and light lace of orange zest.

Serves: 6 to 8

Cappuccino Tortoni

When Chefs Main and Lucas expanded the dining area in The ARK several years ago, they had two large booths custom-built near the south end of the dining area. Since that time, these stunning booths, handcrafted of fir, stained in a rich cherry, and trimmed with leaded glass, have developed a special following of customers, a history of their own. They have become the tables of choice for many of the ARK regulars celebrating anniversaries, birthdays, marriage proposals and other sorts of quiet, intimate celebrations. One couple still likes to reminisce about the time they celebrated the purchase of their new home by ordering an extra dessert "for the table"—a Cappuccino Tortoni, what else?

macaroons
espresso
instant espresso
whipping cream
powdered sugar
kahlua
vanilla
egg whites
salt

Tortoni

Soak **½ c macaroon crumbs** in **3 T espresso*** into which **1 T instant espresso** has been dissolved.

Whip **1 c cream** on medium speed till it begins to thicken. Reduce mixer speed to low and slowly add **½ c sifted powdered sugar.** Then add **3 T kahlua, 1 t vanilla** in a slow stream, mixing till the cream is firm but not dry.

Whip **3 egg whites** till opaque. Add **pinch of salt.** Beat till firm but not glossy.

Fold ⅓ of egg mixture into whipped cream mixture.* Fold in remainder of mixture. Fold in macaroon crumbs.

Spoon in parfait or wine glasses.* Cover each serving tightly with plastic wrap and freeze at least 3 hours.

Topping

Beat **1 c whipping cream** for 1 minute at medium speed. Add **1 T powdered sugar, 2 T kahlua, ¼ t vanilla.** Beat till just thickened. Cream should make soft peaks but still be pourable.

To serve, place dollop of topping on each serving.

T   I   P   S

In place of espresso, you may substitute strong coffee with 1½ T instant coffee stirred in.

It's important to work fast so that egg mixture doesn't fall.

May be presented in 1½ quart glass bowl, served with whipped cream and garnished with whole macaroons or a sprinkle of instant coffee or several chocolate covered espresso beans.

Serves: 6

ESPRESSO ICE CREAM

For a unique surprise, serve sundaes with espresso ice cream and garlic genache sauce,* garnished with a candied rose petal.*

semisweet chocolate
half & half
powdered espresso
water
sugar
egg whites
cream of tartar
whipping cream
vanilla

Stirring often, heat over medium low heat in heavy sauce pan **8 oz semisweet shredded chocolate** in **1 c half & half** till melted and thickened. Add **½ oz powdered instant espresso coffee;** mix well. Let cool, stirring occasionally.

Bring to soft ball stage (235°) **⅓ c water** with **1 c sugar.** Meanwhile, beat **3 egg whites** to stiff peaks, adding **¼ t cream of tartar** when they begin to stiffen. Continue to beat, while pouring sugar syrup in slow stream into whipped egg whites. Continue to beat at medium high speed till mixture is cool.

Fold in cooled chocolate mixture.

Whip **1 c whipping cream** to soft peaks. Fold in **1 T vanilla.** Add cream mixture to egg-chocolate mixture, folding in carefully.

Transfer to freezer trays; put in freezer. When half frozen, remove and hand whip to thick slush; return to freezer trays. Freeze till firm.

T I P S

For garlic genache recipe, see p. 197.

For candied rose technique, see p. 35.

Yield: 1 quart

WHITE CHOCOLATE ICE CREAM

Don't miss the chance to try this refrigerator ice cream.

white chocolate
lemons
water
Midori liqueur
egg yolks
sugar
cream of tartar
whipping cream

Melt **6 oz white chocolate.** Slowly add **juice of 2 lemons, grated peel of 1 lemon, ½ c water** to melted chocolate. Cool; add **⅓ c Midori liqueur.***

Beat **5 egg yolks** until light.

Combine **¼ c water, ½ c sugar,** and **¼ t cream of tartar** and heat to soft ball stage (235°). With yolks beating at high speed, add syrup in a thin stream. Beat for about 5 minutes, until mixture is cool. Add chocolate mixture.

Beat **3 c whipping cream** into soft stage. Fold 1 c of chocolate mixture into cream. Then add this mixture back into the chocolate. Fold till completely incorporated.

Freeze overnight.

T I P S

Amaretto or Grand Marnier may be substituted for Midori.

Yield: 2 quarts

LEMON-PEACH PARFAIT

A drive from downtown Ocean Park to Nahcotta—a scant mile and a half—might take a person from chilly fog rolling in off the ocean into sunshine sparkling across the Bay. On the west side of the peninsula, the ocean can be gray and heavy hung with mists and clouds, the air cool and damp—a hot chocolate kind of day, while on the bay, the sky is blue, the fir trees on Long Island deep rich green, and the coastal range in the distance a gentle gray-brown—picnic weather. The two sides of the peninsula present two different worlds, the one lush and varied, and, except for storms, gentle. The other, the ocean side, stark and simple—dunes covered with straw colored grass, steel gray sand stretching out to the slate gray ocean. But no matter where you are, an ARK dessert makes it even better.

lemon rind
lemon juice
sugar
flour
butter
salt
egg whites
heavy cream
peaches
raspberry puree

Blend **2 T grated lemon rind, ⅓ c fresh lemon juice, ¾ c sugar, 1 T flour, 1 T butter** and a **dash salt** in a small saucepan. Bring to boil. Reduce heat and let simmer 3 to 5 minutes until thickened, stirring occasionally. Let sit 5 minutes.

Meanwhile beat **2 egg whites** until stiff but not dry. Transfer hot liquid to large bowl. Fold whites into liquid a third at a time using a spatula, not a whip. Cool at room temperature.

Whip **1 c heavy cream** until it holds soft peaks. Incorporate into lemon mixture. Chill until firm.

Using about half of the mixture, pipe into bottoms of 6 parfait glasses. Layer peeled **poached fresh peach slices*** over lemon mixture. Dribble **raspberry puree*** over peach layer. Repeat with layer of lemon mixture, layer of peach slices, and drizzling of raspberry puree.

Garnish with white chocolate rosette, a lemon round, and a sprig of fresh mint.

T I P S

For poached peaches, see p. 190. For a variation, used poached pears or sauteed apples.

For raspberry puree, see p. 191.

Yield: 6 generous servings

GATEAU ALLARD NORTHWEST

This Gateau Allard is Chef Main's version of a French recipe that is intended as a homage to fresh raspberries. The original recipe calls for white bread but this Northwest adaptation is unbeatable.

sour cream
vanilla
beaver bread
raspberries
sugar
brown sugar

Line a 10 inch spring form pan with plastic wrap. Criss-cross 2 sheets of wrap so that the whole inside of the pan is covered with at least 6 inches overlapping on each edge since you will be covering the top of the assembled gateau with the wrap. Make sure that the wrap fits flush down into the edges of the pan.

Whisk together **4 c sour cream*** and **1 t vanilla.**

Remove crusts from **2 loaves beaver bread*** and cut the loaf lengthwise into slices ½ inch thick. Fit the slices around the sides of the pan (It's okay to cut to fit.) and then fit slices into the bottom of pan. Be sure all surfaces are covered. (You may use scraps.)

With an elbow spatula, cover the bread thickly with about 1 c sour cream-vanilla mixture. Cover the bottom of this layer with about **1 pint of fresh raspberries.** Sprinkle **½ c white sugar** over berries.*

Spread the sour cream mixture on one side of sliced bread and cover the berry/sugar layer with bread, sour cream side down. Now spread layer of sour cream, then **½ c raspberries,** then ½ c sugar, then bread, sour cream side down as before.

Bring the plastic wrap up over the top of the gateau and wrap tightly. Place a plate or the bottom of another spring form pan on top of the gateau and place a heavy weight on top of that. The weight will force the juice out of the berries as the gateau chills overnight.

After the gateau has chilled overnight, remove it from the pan and unwrap. Ice the top and sides with **2 c sour cream.** Sprinkle about **½ c brown sugar** over the top of the gateau and return it to the refrigerator. The brown sugar will dissolve into the sour cream.

T I P S

For a low-fat version, substitute yogurt after draining excess fluid.

For Beaver Bread recipe, see p. 70.

The sugar will draw the juice out of the berries.

To serve, prepare a raspberry puree. (See p. 191.) Slice the gateau and serve in a pool of raspberry puree with a sour cream sauce made by mixing 2 c sour cream, ¼ c brown sugar and 2 t vanilla or framboise. Stir the sauce until the sugar dissolves and pour it over the gateau. Garnish each slice with three raspberries and a mint leaf.

POPPY SEED TORTE

Chef Main first served this torte for the special ARK anniversary dinner of a couple for whom she had made the wedding cake. Her creative genius seems to blossom when an occasion presents itself. Now you can enjoy this very special cake.

poppy seeds
milk
lemon rind
orange rind
amaretto
whole wheat flour
dry milk
salt
nutmeg
baking powder
eggs
oil
sugar
glucose
water
unsalted butter
simple syrup

Cake

Oven: 350°

Soak **¼ c poppy seeds** in **1 c milk** at room temperature for 45 minutes. Add **1 t lemon rind, 1 t orange rind, 2 T amaretto.** Combine **2 c whole wheat flour, ¼ c dry milk, ½ t salt, pinch nutmeg, 2½ t baking powder.**

Beat **2 eggs** with **¾ c oil** for 3 minutes. Gradually add **1½ c sugar.**

Add portions of liquid and dry mixtures alternately to egg and sugar mixture until completely combined.

Divide into three equal parts and pour into 3 well-greased 8" round cake pans. Bake for 18 to 22 minutes until done.

Buttercream Frosting

Combine **2 c sugar, 2 T glucose,** * ½ c water** in 2 quart sauce pan, using pastry brush to wash down sides of pan with water.

Meanwhile beat **4 eggs** till frothy, with mixer on high.

When sugar-water mixture reaches 235° or soft ball stage, slowly add to eggs in thin stream, continue to beat on high until cool.

Reduce speed to medium and slowly add **1¼ lbs cold unsalted butter** cut into small chunks. As you add chunks one at a time, the mixture will look curdled but it will eventually smooth out.*

Assembly

Freeze layers. Slice each cake layer in half making 2 layers from each, 6 altogether. Place the first layer on cake plate, brush with **1 c simple syrup*** to which **¼ c amaretto** has been added. Spread thin layer of frosting over first layer. Repeat for each subsequent layer. Trim sides. Frost top and sides of cake. Chill before serving.

T I P S

Corn syrup may be substituted for glucose.

Buttercream freezes well. Thaw then beat till smooth. Don't overbeat since too much air in the buttercream makes it spread less well. If buttercream gets too soft to spread, refrigerate it again.

For simple syrup recipe, see p. 35.

CHOCOLATE MINT TRUFFLE TORTE

Don't let the length of this recipe put you off. Take the time to prepare the various parts ahead of time and you'll be rewarded with a total chocolate dessert.

And if you should be lucky enough to take a bite of this Chocolate Mint Truffle Torte at the ARK, you may not realize it, but probably that torte came from the hands of one of the Ark's most valued workers. A lifetime local resident, Rose more or less grew up in The Shake Shack, her mother's tiny restaurant in Ocean Park. The whole peninsula knows about Erna's Buttermilk Pies; in fact, Chef Main takes her own mother there when she comes to visit.

It's not too surprising then to find Rose up to her elbows in flour in the Bakery of the ARK. Watching her form French bread loaves is a treat especially when you hear her story of her first months in the bakery. Rose was sure she'd never make a perfect French bread loaf; now she's happy to instruct the novice in the proper thumb motion for tucking the loaf together. Rose's skill in the bakery was really tested when she was chosen to prepare the dessert tray for Nanci and Jimella's fifth business anniversary celebration.

unsweetened chocolate
unsalted butter
margarine
coffee
flour
baking soda
salt
sugar
buttermilk
eggs
vanilla

Cake

Oven: 400°

Melt **4 oz unsweetened chocolate, ¼ c butter, ¼ c margarine** in **1 c coffee.** Cool.

Sift **2 c all purpose flour.** Re-sift with **1½ t baking soda, 1½ t salt, 2 c sugar.**

In mixing bowl, add dry ingredients to chocolate mixture. Beat together at medium speed, scraping sides of bowls regularly. Add **½ c buttermilk** gradually and beat for 1 minute more. Add **2 beaten eggs.** Beat for 30 seconds. Stir in **1 t vanilla.**

genache

peppermint extract

glucose

water

heavy cream

simple syrup

brandy or cognac

unsweetened cocoa

Divide mixture into 3 greased and floured 8" round cake pans. Bake for 18-20 minutes, until tester comes out clean. Allow the layers to cool; then wrap in plastic wrap. Freeze.

Chocolate-mint genache

Whip **2 c genache.*** Add ¼ **t peppermint extract** (more to taste).

Chocolate buttercream

Combine **2 c sugar, 2 T glucose,*** ½ **c water** in 2 quart sauce pan using pastry brush to wash down sides of pan with water.

Meanwhile, beat **4 eggs** till frothy, mixer on high.

When mixture reaches 235° or soft ball stage, slowly add to eggs in thin stream, continue to beat on high until cool.

Reduce speed to medium and slowly add **1¼ lbs cold unsalted butter*** cut into small chunks. As you add chunks one at a time, the mixture will look curdled but it will eventually smooth out.

Add **2 c genache, 1 t vanilla.** Mix well.*

Chocolate Pastry Cream

In a heavy sauce pan, combine **2 T flour** with ½ **c heavy cream.** When the flour and cream are well-incorporated, add another ½ **c heavy cream.** Add ½ **t salt** and

(continued)

½ **c sugar.** Cook over medium heat till thick. Then whisk **4 egg yolks** till lemon colored. Whisk small amount of hot sauce into yolks. Now whisk yolks back into cream mixture. Return to medium heat. Stir continuously till thick. Remove from heat. Stir in **1 t vanilla.** Remove mixture to mixing bowl and place **1 T soft butter** in small chunks on top. It will melt into mix.

Chocolate mint truffle torte assembly

Slice frozen layers in half, leveling off rounded tops. Brush first layer with **simple syrup*** that has been combined with **2 T brandy or cognac.** Spread **chocolate mint genache** evenly over first layer to a thickness of about 1/8".

Pipe a ¼" thick circle of **chocolate butter cream** around top outside edge of cake. Spread **chocolate pastry cream** evenly inside circle over top of layer. Top with next layer.

Repeat process four more times. Chill assembled torte for at least 15 minutes before frosting.

Frost top and sides of torte with **butter cream.** Chill 15 minutes. Frost again using hot, dry spatula. Using a star tip decorate with buttercream rosettes.

Top with **12 truffles*** made by dividing
½ c chilled genache into 12 equal parts and
rolling into balls. Set the balls out on a flat
surface, freeze, then roll in unsweetened
cocoa.

T I P S
▼

For genache recipe see p. 197, omit garlic
honey.

Corn syrup may be substituted for glucose.

It is very important that the butter be cold.

Buttercream freezes well. Thaw and beat till
smooth. Don't overbeat since too much air in
the buttercream makes it spread less well. If
buttercream gets too soft to spread, refrigerate
it again.

For simple syrup recipe, see p. 35.

These truffles, incredibly rich candies, can be
flavored with any number of liqueurs and
eaten by themselves.

A major breakthrough in oyster raising occurred when a man named Bill Budge discovered that oysters in the larval stage could be removed from the water for hours and could be kept out of the water for up to a week if they were kept cool and moist. This discovery made it possible to move oysters fertilized in a hatchery to a grower before they are attached to cultch. The great advantage here is the size of the oysters being moved. One million oyster larvae weigh ⅔ of an ounce; attached to cultch they could weigh over a ton. A million larvae now would require only the space occupied by a cherry tomato; before, attached to cultch, they would have filled a standard size pick-up truck.

NOTES

Ark
Special Sauces

LIFE ON A CONCRETE BOAT

Just to the south of the ARK, on the tide flats in the bay, Larry and Marge tend an oyster bed. That in itself is not so unusual. Nor is it particularly strange that they work the beds on a shared profit basis with the owner. But a visitor to the ARK, seeing Larry or Marge head out on foot to the racks of oysters when the tide is out, gets just the first inkling of how these people and their oysters are different.

Marge and Larry live in a concrete shell boat which they built over the rusting hull of a metal boat that they got for "the towing away." The boat sits on the tide flat south of the ARK, out of the water during all but the highest tides and wildest storms. The boat looks for all the world like an overgrown kayak with three seats instead of one or two.

As diners look to the south, they see, about 30 yards from the boat, black stakes sticking up out of the bay—those stakes hold either net bags with growing oysters in them or lines with the oysters ingeniously woven into them. This method keeps the oysters up off the bottom, floating in the water, filtering the nutrients from the water as it moves around them. The oysters grow faster, fatter and tastier this way. Larry and Marge walk out to the beds during low tide, pick the oysters, wash them, bag them, put them in a small two wheeled wagon and deliver them to the restaurant.

Talking to them gives the cliche, "They know what they're doing," a new dimension. They burn waste for heat; the heat warms the inside of their home as well as water for washing or making tea. They get electricity from a windmill, hot water from the sun, fertilizer for their garden from the silt washed off the oysters. They concentrate on producing more energy than they use and try to help others do the same.

RED PEPPER SAUCE

This sauce is as beautiful as it is tasty. Its bright red color provides a suitable preface to its rich, spicy flavor.

butter
red bell peppers
garlic
tomatoes
madeira
raspberry vinegar
chili pepper
red currant jelly
brown sugar

Place into saucepan **¼ lb butter, 6 chopped red bell peppers, 1 T minced garlic, 4 coarsely chopped tomatoes.** Cook over medium high heat for 20 minutes until vegetables break down.

Add **2 T madeira, ¼ c raspberry vinegar*** and **4½ t chili pepper.** Cook for 1 to 3 minutes. Add **1 c red currant jelly, ½ c brown sugar.** Cook 5 to 10 minutes until ingredients fully integrate.

Puree mixture in food processor. Pass through china cap or seive.

T I P S

For raspberry vinegar recipe, see p. 193.
Yield: 3 cups

PEPPER PAN SAUCE

Put this sauce heated over baked salmon, tangy omelets, or vegetarian casseroles. It makes wonderful mock spanish rice and gives a whole new dimension to snapper. It freezes well and will keep refrigerated for weeks. If you have it on hand you will find your own uses for this tangy, bright sauce.

green peppers
onions
parsley
butter
black pepper
garlic
tabasco
tomato sauce
chili sauce

Finely chop then saute **4 green peppers, 2 medium onions, 2 T chopped parsley with stems** in ¼ **c clarified butter*** for 20 minutes at medium high heat.

Add **1 T black pepper, 1½ T minced garlic, 2 T tabasco.** Add **3 qts tomato sauce,* 5 c chili sauce.** Bring to rumbling boil, turn down to simmering rumble.

Cook uncovered for 45 minutes, stirring frequently.

T I P S

For clarified butter technique, see p. 34.

For tomato sauce recipe, see p. 180.

Yield: 4 quarts

CURRY SAUCE

If you're dining at the ARK and happen to notice a waitress who looks a bit more longingly at the water than most, you've caught Cheri with visions of sailing dancing before her eyes. You see, when Cheri's not waiting tables at the ARK, she's finishing a 36 foot boat that she and a friend have been building for some years now. Her commitment to the ARK represents the current chapter of a rich and varied life.

A major in communication and psychology at the University of Tennessee, she "never quite decided whether to go to law school," so, after finishing college, Cheri worked in a mountain resort there. Next, she managed to land a job cooking for an atmospheric research team in Antarctica for five months. There, the only living things besides the 50 or so humans were whales, gulls, and penguins. "When we finally got to Christchurch, there was a dead bug in the bathroom and everybody got all excited," she remembers. Now, here she is serving at one of the finest restaurants in the country while she spends her other hours under a plastic dome that cover a 36 foot nearly finished sailboat. Someday, when her ARK chapter closes, Cheri will sail away to the San Juan Islands, Mexico, and, ultimately, Hawaii.

apples
carrots
onions
celery
parsley
garlic
butter
bay leaves
fennel seed
coriander
curry
dry mustard

Coarsely chop **5 red delicious apples, 2 carrots, 2 medium onions, 3 ribs celery, ½ bunch parsley.** Press **1 head garlic.** Add vegetables to **½ lb butter** in stock pot; saute for 30 minutes, stirring constantly.

After 30 minutes, add mixture of **2 bay leaves, 3 t fennel seed, 1 T coriander, 2 to 3 T curry, 1 T dry mustard, 1½ t mace, 2 t nutmeg, 1½ t allspice, 1 chopped hot pepper pod.*** Cook 3 to 5 minutes, stirring constantly.

Add **1 qt fish stock.*** Cook for 20 to 25 minutes.

mace	Remove from heat; allow to cool to warm, then, while still warm, run through food processor and pass through china cap or colander. Press through with wooden spoon.
nutmeg	
allspice	
pepper pod	
fish stock	Cool, then refrigerate.

T I P S

Use any of the following peppers: 1 Santaka pepper, 1 Anaheim, 1 New Mexican, or 2 jalapeno.

For fish stock recipe, see p. 194. Fish bouillon may be substituted.

Yield: 5 cups

The oysters most of us eat are between two and five years old when they're the tastiest. But if they're not attacked by any of their natural enemies, oysters can live for as long as fifty years. The Willapa Bay Marine Biology lab has a twenty-five pound oyster in its collection.

TERIYAKI SAUCE

A hundred years or more ago, two Indians in a canoe could find a sturgeon on the shoals, hook it with a pole, race with it till the fish tired, stun it with a club, and then with a quick jerk of the line flip the mighty creature into the canoe without ever turning the boat or damaging the fish.

People fishing the Columbia River, today, catch sturgeon, but everything under three or over six feet long must be thrown back. Sturgeon can grow to twelve or fifteen feet; they can weigh as much as 400 pounds—not something caught with a stick, a string, and a bent pin.

The real enjoyment of the sturgeon comes, though, when it gets prepared ARK-style with this teriyaki sauce to make Chef Lucas's menu standard, Sturgeon Szechwan.

garlic	Blend together **4 t minced fresh garlic,**
ginger	**2 t minced fresh ginger, 1 c soy sauce,**
soy sauce	**⅔ c sherry, juice of 2 lemons,**
sherry	**½ c brown sugar, 2 to 3 T honey.** Before using, stir up from bottom.
lemons	
brown sugar	This sauce will keep refrigerated up to 1 month.
honey	
	Yield: 2 cups

PESTO SAUCE

This classic sauce keeps well; make large batches when basil is in season, then freeze it. Simply pour on a topping of olive oil and cover tightly.

garlic	Chop in food processor or blender **4 to 5 cloves garlic.**
basil	
parsley	With machine off, pack tightly **2½ c cleaned fresh basil.** Chop fine.
pine nuts	
parmesan	Add **1/8 c fresh parsley.** Chop fine.
salt	Add **¼ c pine nuts, ¼ c freshly grated parmesan cheese, ½ t salt.** Blend.
olive oil	

Add slowly, with machine running, **½ c olive oil** till it forms a smooth paste.

Yield: 1 cup

SESAME-POPPY SEED SAUCE

The bottle collections that can be found all up and down the peninsula provide a record of an earlier day. One of the most complete can be seen in the windows of John Crellin's 1893 house in Oysterville. The medicine flasks remind us that though hospitals were not among the early amenities, some help was available for the sick. The hand-blown eight-sided ink bottles tell us that from the beginning there were schools; in 1863 Oysterville established the first public school in Pacific County. And the large number of liquor containers are clear evidence of the five saloons that flourished in Oysterville's heyday.

Most of the bottles are turned up in gardens where pioneer houses and stores once stood. The ocean side, on the other hand, has provided this century's beachcombers with another kind of glass—round, palegreen, or blue glass fishnet floats that come in on the current all the way from Japan. The very rare purple glass floats were used by the Royal Fishing Fleet of that country. Some are very small, only a few inches, but others can be as large as twenty inches in diameter. Many big ones have been made into lamp bases by those who have been eager enough to go down to find them after storms.

poppy seeds *garlic*	Run **1½ T poppy seeds** in food processor for 15 seconds.
green onions *dijon mustard*	Add **5 cloves garlic, 6 chopped green onions.** Run processor for 30 more seconds.
lemon *brown sugar* *raspberry wine vinegar*	Add **1 T dijon mustard, juice of three lemons, 2 T brown sugar, 4 T raspberry wine vinegar.*** Run processor for 30 seconds.
vegetable oil *sesame oil* *egg*	Slowly pour mixture of **1½ c vegetable oil** plus **½ c sesame oil** into processor while it runs.
	Drop in **1 egg;** mix for 10 seconds.
	Refrigerate.

T I P S

For raspberry vinegar recipe, see p. 193.

This sauce will keep well for a month in the refrigerator.

Use this sauce on crab meat, oysters, or as a spread for turkey sandwiches. Let your imagination lead you.

Yield: 1 quart

Twenty years ago the remnants of at least four shipwrecked vessels could be seen on the driving beach between the Fishing Rocks at the south end of the peninsula and Leadbetter Point at the north, most of them wooden-hulled since steel distintegrates faster than wood in salt water. Now the shifting sand has covered them all.

In the last ten years residents have watched the disappearance of the wreckage of a tuna boat that ran aground in 1976 on the beach south of the Cape Disappointment Light.

ELEGANT CHEESE SAUCE

At the ARK, you will find this sauce as part of the perennial favorite Crab Kasseri. But Chef Lucas is quite proud of this versatile sauce and encourages home chefs to experiment with it. You can't go wrong.

milk	Bring to high heat in double boiler **4 c milk,**
salt	**¼ t salt, pinch white pepper, 1 T dry**
white pepper	**mustard, 6 shakes tabasco.**
dry mustard	When it is quite hot, add **6 to 7 T roux.***
tabasco	Let cook for 5 to 10 minutes till it thickens.
roux	Melt into mixture **½ c grated parmesan**
parmesan	**cheese, ¾ c sharp cheddar.**
sharp cheddar	After cheese melts, add **¼ c sherry** and
sherry	**¼ c beer.**
beer	

T I P S

For roux recipe see p. 34.

Do not allow top pan to touch boiling water in bottom pan.

For best results use the sharpest aged cheddar you can find.

Sauce should rest before using—at least come to room temperature.

For a vegetarian dinner, saute your favorite vegetables, place in casserole dish, top with cheese sauce, bake at 375° for 10 minutes.

For a tasty scallop entree, bring to boil mixture of 4 c fish stock, 2 c wine, one lemon. Gently poach scallops for 3 to 5 minutes. Remove from liquid and place in casserole dish. Cover with cheese sauce and sprinkle parmesan on top. Bake at 425° for 10 to 12 minutes.

If you prefer prawns, saute 3 or 4 prawns lightly with 2 to 4 T clarified butter. Add ½ c sliced mushrooms, ¼ c sliced green onions. Deglaze with cognac. Place in casserole dish, top with cheese sauce and loosely shredded parmesan. Bake at 425° for 10 to 12 minutes.

Yield: 1½ quarts

TOMATO SAUCE

Tomato Sauce is basic to many recipes, and Chef Lucas's new version should become a staple in every kitchen.

butter
garlic
scallions
carrot
bay leaf
thyme
basil
oregano
salt
pepper
roma or plum
tomatoes
dry vermouth

Saute briefly in **2 T butter, 1 to 2 cloves minced garlic, 2 minced scallion bulbs, 1 finely chopped carrot, 1 bay leaf, ¼ t thyme, ¼ t basil, ¼ t oregano, salt, pepper** to taste.

Add **5 lbs diced roma** or **plum tomatoes, ¾ c dry vermouth.** Bring to boil, simmer gently no more than one hour.

Pass through sieve, remove bay leaf, cool to room temperature, refrigerate.

Yield: 1½ quarts

GINO SAUCE

A brief run down of some of the fine food sources indigenous to the Long Beach Peninsula region makes it easy to understand how the ARK chefs are regularly inspired to new taste combinations. Chef Lucas regularly works with Dungeness crab, Chinook salmon, Willapa Bay oysters, Columbia River sturgeon, and butter clams from Long Island in the Bay just east of the restaurant. Her Gino Sauce uses Dungeness crab and is often served on her specialty Oysters Gino made with Willapa Bay oysters.

bacon	Fry **1 thin slice bacon** in **1 t butter** till brown.
butter	
garlic	Add **1 t chopped garlic, ¼ t chopped parsley, 2 shakes tabasco, salt, pepper** to taste, **juice of 1 wedge of lemon, 1 c crab meat.*** Saute.
parsley	
tabasco	
salt	
pepper	Deglaze with **⅓ c madeira.** Set aside.
lemon	Heat **⅓ c fish stock,* 1 c half & half.**
crab	When hot, nearly boiling, add **2 T roux.*** Mix till thickened.
madeira	
fish stock	Add **¾ c parmesan.** When cooked in, add **¼ c sherry.**
half & half	
roux	Fold into crab mixture and refrigerate.
parmesan	
sherry	

T I P S

Use Dungeness crab meat if possible.

For fish stock recipe, see p. 194; fish bouillon may be substituted.

For roux recipe, see p. 34.

Yield: 2 cups

HOLLANDAISE SAUCE

Once you've learned the technique of hollandaise sauce, you're ready for anything in the kitchen.

egg yolks
tabasco
salt
white pepper
worcestershire
dry vermouth
clarified butter
lemon

While heating double boiler, whisk vigorously **4 egg yolks** with **1 dash tabasco, salt** and **white pepper** to taste, **1 dash worcestershire, 2 T dry vermouth.**

When the sauce turns pale and the whisk marks appear, remove from heat and drizzle in **¾ c to 1 c clarified butter*** at just above room temperature.

Whisk till stiff; add juice of **½ lemon.**

T I P S

The top pan should not sit in the water in the lower pan.

For clarified butter technique, see p. 34.

Keep ice water handy; if sauce starts to break, add drops of water.

Yield: about 1 cup.

HUCKLEBERRY SAUCE

Old timers on the peninsula remember picking wild red huckleberries from the bushes along the old train tracks. Nowadays, the Chefs at the ARK rely, for their berries, on pickers who have staked out secret patches of berry bushes to which they return each year.

huckleberries	Mash and strain enough huckleberries to
sugar	produce **1 c huckleberry juice.**
cornstarch	In a heavy sauce pan, wisk together **½ c**
orange juice	**sugar, 4 t cornstarch.**
butter	Blend in huckleberry juice and **½ c orange**
lemon juice	**juice.** Bring to boil and let simmer 1 to 2 minutes till sauce is thick and translucent.
	Remove from heat. Stir in **1 T butter, 2 t lemon juice.**
	Stir in **1 c huckleberries** (be generous).

T I P S

Blueberry sauce and strawberry sauce can be made using this recipe simply by substituting the same quantities of berries for the huckleberries.

Yield: 2 cups

Basics of Ark Cooking

A CLAMMING
WE WILL GO

Every year when the digging season is on, the twenty-eight miles of the ocean shore look like the parking lot for a world series game: cars, pickups, and campers parked side by side from Seaview to Leadbetter Point, the wet sand black with people, armed with long narrow shovels or tubular clam guns, clam licenses pinned to their jackets, stamping the sand in the hope that a little round hole will announce the location of a razor clam.

Clams were plentiful in the old days, when clam-diggers were scarcer. Regulations in the early part of this century required only that clams less than three and a half inches be thrown back and many small ones, their shells broken, died. Some old shovels still have that three-and-a-half inch gauge marked on the handles. Between 1910 and the late 1940's clam canneries flourished on the peninsula, and every tenth house, it seemed, had a hand-lettered sign, "Clams Cleaned Here," for those too lazy or too ignorant to do their own. The giant skillet, six feet in diameter that still hangs on Long Beach's main street is a relic of the clam festivals held in the thirties, when the world's largest clam fritter was fried and distributed free to all comers.

Now the diggers are limited to fifteen clams, if they can find them; every clam must be kept, no matter how small; the open season grows shorter every year. In spite of these efforts at conservation, however, one of the world's greatest delicacies is rapidly disappearing.

GARLIC HONEY

garlic
honey

Peel **1 dozen garlic cloves,** add to
½ c honey. Store in cool dark place for at
least 1 week, no longer than 1 month.

Strain garlic honey through wire mesh
strainer. Store in glass jar.

T I P S

Add garlic honey to teriyaki sauce.

Garlic honey is a wonderful glaze for chicken
and meat.

Make garlic toast with garlic honey.

Yield: ½ cup

ALMOND-GARLIC PRALINE SAUCE

butter
almonds
garlic
parsley
lemon
amaretto

Heat ¼ **c clarified butter*** in saute pan. Add **½ c chopped almonds, ¼ t minced garlic, pinch chopped parsley,** squeeze of **1 wedge of lemon.** Saute until garlic and almonds start to brown.

Deglaze with **⅓ c amaretto.** Cook until syrupy.

T I P S

For clarified butter technique, see p. 34.

Yield: ⅔ cup

POACHED PEACHES

sugar

water

peaches

lemon

Combine **2 c sugar** and **2 c water.** Bring mixture to a boil.

Immerse **whole peaches** in boiling syrup for no more than three minutes.

Remove fruit from boiling liquid and place in ice water. Skins should peel off easily.

Cool syrup mixture to room temperature and then return peeled peaches to this liquid.

Squeeze **1 lemon** over the peaches to prevent them from discoloring. Peaches can be refrigerated in the syrup.

RASPBERRY PUREE

raspberries
sugar
water
lemon

Bring to boil **2 c raspberries, ½ c sugar** in **½ c water.** Remove immediately from heat. Squeeze **1 t lemon juice** into mixture.

Puree mixture in a blender or food processor. Pass through a sieve.

Yield: 2½ cups

he United States Coast Guard operates the country's only heavy surf rescue school at Cape Disappointment at the mouth of the Columbia River. Modern technology has greatly reduced the number of shipwrecks and provided new techniques for this particularly dangerous kind of rescue, but the skill and bravery of the graduates of the Heavy Surf Rescue School are still the difference.

CRANBERRY PUREE

cranberries
water
sugar
grand marnier
orange peel

Boil **1 lb cranberries** in **2 c water.** Add **2 c sugar.** Simmer about 10 minutes or till skins pop.

Run through blender or food processor. Pass through sieve, including pulp.

Add **¼ c grand marnier, 1 t grated orange peel.**

Yield: 2 to 3 cups

BERRY VINEGAR

white vinegar
sugar
berries
garlic

Boil for 10 minutes **4 c white vinegar, ⅓ c sugar, 2 c rinsed berries,* 6 cloves peeled garlic** split to center.

Cool to room temperature, cover tightly, let steep for 2 days.

Strain through cheesecloth. Cover tightly to store.

T I P S

Use strawberries, raspberries, or blueberries.

Use this vinegar on salads, or sprinkle over sliced tomatoes.

Yield: 1 quart

FISH STOCK

water
fish scraps
onion
carrot
fennel
bay leaves
salt
black
peppercorns

Bring to boil **2 to 3 qts water, 1 lb fish scraps,* 1 large onion,** cut up into chunks, **½ to 1 c chopped carrot, ½ to 1 c chopped whole fennel, 2 bay leaves, salt** and **10 peppercorns.**

Simmer about 3 hours, strain through cheesecloth, cool and refrigerate or freeze.

T I P S

For fish scraps, use heads **without gills,** tails, bones and trimmings. Salmon, snapper, halibut work especially well. Do not use sturgeon.

If you prefer a less fishy flavor, add 4 to 6 anise stars.

Yield: 1½ to 2 quarts

CHICKEN STOCK

water
chicken
gizzards
onion
garlic
carrot
celery
parsley
thyme
marjoram
basil
bay leaf
cloves
peppercorns
salt

Bring to boil **3 to 4 quarts cold water.** Add **2 to 3 lbs chicken parts,** and **2 lbs gizzards, 2 c onion, 2 to 3 cloves garlic, 1 to 2 c carrot, 1 to 2 c celery, 1 c parsley, 1 t fresh thyme, ½ t marjoram, 1 t basil, a bay leaf, 4 to 6 cloves, peppercorns** and **salt.**

Cover and simmer 1 to 1½ hours. Taste for seasoning and correct.

Simmer another hour. Strain through cheesecloth and cool. Remove fat and refrigerate or freeze.

Yield: 3 quarts

GARLIC STOCK

garlic
onion
cloves
water
carrots
parsley
bay leaf

Cut bulbs of **1 pound or more of garlic** in half horizontally—as though you were cutting a grapefruit. Peel **1 small onion,** stud it with **6 cloves.** Put garlic and onion into **1½ gallons water;** add **3 cut carrots, 1 c coarsely chopped parsley, 1 bay leaf.** Bring to boil, simmer 1½ to 2 hours uncovered.*

Strain.

T I P S

If a stronger flavor is desired, simmer for an additional 45 minutes and/or use more garlic.

This stock can be used to cook rice, to flavor vegetables, as well as in the garlic rose soup on p. 97.

Yield: 3 quarts

GARLIC GENACHE SAUCE

cream
butter
sugar
chocolate
garlic honey

In heavy saucepan, mix then bring to boil **1 pt heavy cream, ¼ c butter, ¼ c sugar.**

Remove from heat and add **1 lb shredded bittersweet or semisweet chocolate.** Stir till melted.

Add **¼ c garlic honey;*** stir till mixed. Store in refrigerator.

T I P S

For garlic honey recipe, see p. 188.

Serve over espresso ice cream. See p. 148 for recipe.

To use genache in truffles and tortes, omit garlic honey.

Yield: 3 pints

INDEX OF RECIPES

(continued)

INDEX OF INGREDIENTS

(continued)

ACKNOWLEDGEMENTS

Shirley Anderson, Bruce Betz, Kaaren Black, Rich Bohn, Tim Brennan, Jerry Brown, Laura and Doug Busch, Hal Calbrom, Shirley Collins, Kevin Crozier, Tom Darden, Dutch Daut, George and Linda Dewey, Linda and Ed Dodge, Jack and Lucille Downer, Jim and Marie Finlay, Georgia L. Fletcher, Patty Franklin, Jeannie Gammel, Ken Grant, Michael Grigsby, Ella Mae Haar, Robert Haar, Florence Hardcastle, Mary Jo and Don Hessel, Lila and Don Hewitt, Paul Hermann, Ann and Kate Higgins, Helen and Merlyn Hobson, Lonnie Howard, Lyle and Marilyn Janz, Linda Johnson, Phil and Harold Johnson, Marion Johnson, Roy Johnson, Ginger Johnston, Cynthia R. Knock, Sharon Lane, Kathy Lattin, Edith Lotz, Tara McGown, Evelyn and Raymond Main, Margaret and Manuel Main, John and Joan Mann, John Marshall, Ruth Medak, Shirley Nichols, Kaye Norton, Meredith Owens, Ruthann Panowitz, Carol and Steve Payne, Nadene and Pete Peterson, Rose Pike, Kathy Piper, Marty Piper, Mavis and Mick Piper, Erna Preston, Rose Preston, Helen and Joe Prindle, Malinda Pryde, Janet Rose, Frank Ross, Yvonne Rothert, April Ryan, Jim and Diane Rzegocki, Fritz Schlatter, Gordon Schoene, Lillian and Renard Shepard, Julia Smith, Lynn Smith, Bette Snyder, Dave and Ann Stadler, Dewey and Dorothy Tribble, Paul Vandervelt, Charlie Vos, Allison Walker, Brian and Beth Walker, Norma Walker, Hazel Ward, Eva and Fred Werkman, Jennie L. Werremeyer, Kim and Miles Wilcox, Karen Winn, Mary Wright, Ted and Carol Zell.

Eric Griswold, photographer for *Bay and Ocean,*
works primarily in product and food illustration.
He has worked as a photographer for nearly fifteen
years and opened his own business, Griswold
Studios, in Portland, Oregon, four years ago.
Though born in Paris, he has lived most of his life
in the Northwest. "I like it here and wouldn't want
to live anywhere else."

Mark Wiseman, designer of the first ARK
cookbook, *The Ark: Cuisine of the Pacific
Northwest,* repeats as the designer of this second
book from the ARK restaurant. In addition he has
created the original pastel for the book cover.
Wiseman Design of St. Louis, Missouri, has won
advertising and design awards throughout the
country.

ORDERING POSTERS AND BOOKS

The cover of **Bay and Ocean** is an original work of art by
award winning graphic artist Mark Wiseman. A limited number
of **Bay and Ocean** posters are available for purchase at $9.95
(includes postage and handling). These posters of the cover art
measure 17" x 22" and are printed on heavy textured stock.

Further copies of the **Bay and Ocean** cookbook may be
purchased for $21.95 ($19.95 + 2.00 postage and handling).
The coupons opposite may be used to order posters and books.

Please send me_____copies of **Bay and Ocean:
Ark Restaurant Cuisine** at $21.95 each ($19.95 +
2.00 postage and handling). U.S. currency only.   _____

_____copies of the **Bay and Ocean** poster at $9.95
(includes postage and handling). U.S. currency only.   _____

Missouri residents add 6% sales tax.   _____

                                          Total   _____

Makes checks payable to **Ladysmith Ltd., Publishers**
                        P.O. Box 30045
                        St. Louis, MO 63119

Ship to: Name _____
         Address_____
         City _____ State _____ Zip _____

Please send me_____copies of **Bay and Ocean:
Ark Restaurant Cuisine** at $21.95 each ($19.95 +
2.00 postage and handling). U.S. currency only.   _____

_____copies of the **Bay and Ocean** poster at $9.95
(includes postage and handling). U.S. currency only.   _____

Missouri residents add 6% sales tax.   _____

                                          Total   _____

Makes checks payable to **Ladysmith Ltd., Publishers**
                        P.O. Box 30045
                        St. Louis, MO 63119

Ship to: Name _____
         Address_____
         City _____ State _____ Zip _____